God of No Fixed Address

God of No Fixed Address

From Altars to Sanctuaries, Temples to Houses

Jean-Claude Verrecchia

WIPF & STOCK · Eugene, Oregon

GOD OF NO FIXED ADDRESS
From Altars to Sanctuaries, Temples to Houses

God of No Fixed Address: translation and adaptation of the French *Dieu sans domicile fixe*.

Vie et Santé. Dammarie-les-lys, France, 2013.

Copyright © 2015 Jean-Claude Verrecchia. All rights reserved. Except for brief quotations in critical publications or reviews, no part of this book may be reproduced in any manner without prior written permission from the publisher. Write: Permissions, Wipf and Stock Publishers, 199 W. 8th Ave., Suite 3, Eugene, OR 97401.

Wipf & Stock
An Imprint of Wipf and Stock Publishers
199 W. 8th Ave., Suite 3
Eugene, OR 97401

www.wipfandstock.com

ISBN 13: 978-1-4982-0730-0

Manufactured in the U.S.A.

New Revised Standard Version Bible, 1989, Division of Christian Education of the National Council of the Churches of Christ in the United States of America. Used by permission. All rights reserved.

Contents

Introduction: Invitation to Travel | ix

Part 1

Itinerary 1
In the Beginning: God in the Middle of the Garden | 3

Itinerary 2
From Altars to Altars: God Follows the Patriarchs | 6

Itinerary 3
God Settles in the Midst of His People: The Sanctuary of the Desert | 10

Itinerary 4
The Symbolism of the Sanctuary | 20

Itinerary 5
The God Who Eats with His Own; or, Sacrifices in the Old Testament | 32

Itinerary 6
David Wants God to Live in a Temple: From Nomads to Settlers | 47

Itinerary 7
Solomon Builds the Temple . . . and Destroys the Monarchy | 58

Itinerary 8
Jeremiah and Illusory Confidence in the Temple | 69

Itinerary 9
Ezekiel, the Priest Without a Temple | 74

Interlude | 81

Part 2

Prologue | 89

Itinerary 1
God's House in Paul's Letters; or, When God Moves On | 90

Itinerary 2
Mark and the Temple of God—The Torn Curtain | 104

Itinerary 3
From the Temple to Homes: God's Dwelling Place in the Work of Luke | 113

Itinerary 4
The "Epistle" to the Hebrews; or, Invitation to Enter the Sanctuary | 123

Itinerary 5
At Home with John: The Lord Goes Camping | 136

Itinerary 6
The Temple of God in the Book of Revelation | 141

Conclusion: Journey's End | 147

Bibliography | 151

To Mike and Helen Pearson, my translator and editor, without whom the English version of this book would have never appeared.
With my deepest gratitude.

Introduction

Invitation to Travel

TOURISTS, WORLD TRAVELLERS, AND history enthusiasts have seen hundreds of them in all of the great cities of the world as well as in unexpected corners of small villages: commemorative plaques which tell us that a famous person lived in a certain place. One of the most amusing commemorative plaques is to be seen in the town of Digne-les-Bains in Provence, France: "Napoleon I, on his return from the island of Elba, paused here from noon to three o'clock on 4th March 1815." A plaque for a three-hour stay! Knowing where famous people lived—kings and princes, presidents and ministers, artists and indeed all those who make the news—is more significant than it might seem. The tabloid press has grasped this very well and publishes photos, from official sources or paparazzi, of the homes of celebrities. To know where someone lives, to be able to visualize their natural habitat is to experience a degree of intimacy with them. It is to share a little part of their life. It is to enter their inner circle. On the other hand, people who conceal their address may well arouse suspicion.

And what of God? Where does God live? There is no commemorative plaque for him. In Capernaum, beside the Sea of Galilee, modern pilgrims can see what was probably the house where the Apostle Peter lived, but there is no such specific place which Jesus could have called home—fortunately. The pious might locate God in heaven. Some of the faithful would have him in a cathedral.

Introduction

Some would say he was in his sanctuary. Others would claim he was everywhere in nature. Still others would counter that he is nowhere. Asking where God lives is not an idle question. Does God live nearby or far away? Does he occupy one place or is he always on the move? Can anyone visit God's dwelling place—and if so what are the entry requirements? Or is it a place completely off limits to humans? The purpose of this book is to answer such questions. I have entered into the satnav of my research the following instruction: Go to the house of God. But we all know full well that such navigation gadgets never offer a single itinerary. The biblical GPS is no different. It provides a list of possible routes. I have decided to explore a substantial number of them but not all of them because the journey would be far too long.

By now you will have realized that for this book, as far as possible, I have chosen to use everyday language. Purposely, Bible references are given in the footnotes only and Bible verses are fully quoted in the main text.

This book does not tell you what you should believe or not believe, what you should do or should not do. Instead, I hope you will see it as one of those guidebooks for intelligent travellers who don't want to return quite the same people they were as when they set out.

It remains only for me to wish you a good trip as you go in search of the house of God. Travel in several directions, follow several routes, and enjoy the trip.

PART 1

Itinerary 1

In the Beginning

God in the Middle of the Garden

From the very first lines of the book of Genesis, God speaks: to the light, to the firmament—the great sky vault—to the waters, to the heavenly bodies, to the animals and to the other living beings. And then finally to human beings. To them God speaks in the first person: "See, I have given you every plant yielding seed that is upon the face of all the earth,"[1] for in this creation human beings have a place of honor. They are the crowning glory of creation, its very reason for existing. "No polite fussiness between you and me, says God, we are on first name terms." "You may freely eat of every tree of the garden."[2]

When things go wrong in the relationship, God does not take refuge behind his offended dignity leaving human beings to their miserable lot. He might easily have gone red in the face with anger. But not so. He stays close by them to stay in contact with them: "Where are you?"[3] he calls. Was he disappointed? Undoubtedly. Overcome with sadness? Of course but not to the point of breaking their close relationship. God goes looking for Adam and Eve:

1. Gen 1:29.
2. Gen 2:17.
3. Gen 3:10.

"They heard the sound of the Lord God walking in the garden at the time of the evening breeze."[4] In spite of all this the conversation will continue: between "I" and "you." "*I* was afraid . . . the woman whom *you* gave to be with me . . . *I* ate."[5]

The opening lines of the Bible relating the story dwell at length on the presence of God. He is there. He speaks. He discusses. He asks questions. God is right in the center of the garden, up close to those whom he has created, particularly after their first disobedience. The God of the Bible has this on his visiting card:

GOD
Creator

Address: Garden of Eden—Center
Hours of Operation: 24/7 without exception, Sunday to Saturday.

This God who is present, who is in our midst, contrasts sharply with those other gods in ancient Near East stories of the creation of the world written before the book of Genesis. These gods are far away from the one who wishes to be with his creation and to talk to it. These gods—Apsu, Tiamat, Lakmu, Marduk, to name but a few—fight with each other. And as we all know, war carries a high cost. For them the creation of man has no other purpose than to ensure supply to their demands. Marduk says: "I will create man who shall inhabit the earth, that the service of the gods may be established, and that their shrines may be built."[6] The

---

4. Gen 3:8.
5. Gen 3:12–13.
6. *Emuna Elish*, VI.

priests are in charge of washing, clothing, feeding and entertaining the gods.

There is nothing like this in the Bible. Human beings are not there simply to do the bidding of God. Quite the opposite—rather it is God who is at the service of the humans whom he has created. And to achieve this, nothing works better than living side by side with them. In the final vision which brings the biblical canon to a close, John sees a new heaven and a new earth and hears a voice saying loud and clear: "See, the home of God is among mortals. He will dwell with them as their God; they will be his peoples, and God himself will be with them."[7] Right from the beginning in Eden God had decided to live among the creatures of his hand, among human beings. But the error of Adam and Eve had made his preference impossible. Once the problem of the first mistake had been righted, what was more logical than for God to settle in the midst of his own family? Back to square one!

So in the meantime, between the first and last pages of the Bible, is God consigned to absence and to silence? Absolutely not. In the following pages we will analyze certain key passages which show the many and varied attempts of God to stay with us against all the odds.

---

7. Rev 21:3.

ITINERARY 2

From Altars to Altars

God Follows the Patriarchs

GOD'S EXCLUSION OF HUMAN beings from the garden was not so much a punishment but rather a protection from the worst consequences of what they had done. If they have stayed in the garden they would have been endlessly condemned to re-experience the results of their actions. For women the pains of childbirth would have gone on and on and on. Forever, they would have had to accept without question the dominance of the so-called stronger sex. For men, work would have been endless, without respite, without hope of a break. Inherent in the expulsion from the garden was the promise of something better some day. Paradoxically it was ejection from the garden which brought hope. Deprived of unlimited access to the tree of life which would have made Adam and Eve both terminally and eternally ill, now they can be reborn. After the dust has settled, human beings will rise from the ashes. Strangely enough exclusion from the garden of Eden opens the way to future admission to the heavenly Jerusalem.

God himself stays in the garden! And the human beings whom he has created stay strictly outside. And it's not only Cain who "went away from the presence of God"[1] but all human beings.

1. Gen 4:16.

The account later drawn up about God is alarming: "The Lord saw that the wickedness of humankind was great in the earth, and that every inclination of the thoughts of their hearts was only evil continually."[2] His decision is taken: "I will blot out from the earth the human beings I have created,"[3] says God. But it is difficult to imagine him as an abusive father. Just as he excels in his role as creator and as a loving father, so he struggles with matters of punishment and destruction. What is the Bible but an endless catalogue of stories in which God threatens to mete out well-deserved punishment and then changes his mind and offers grace and forgiveness?

At the same time as he is planning to put his whole creation in the great washing machine of the flood, God is scouring the world in search of a family who would go through the whole cycle. He settles on Mr. and Mrs. Noah and their three sons. A fine family certainly. "I will destroy everything in sight, says God, except . . . except these people, for I would like to rerun the experiment." This God is a world champion at new beginnings. With him it is never over. Everything can always start again. "God remembered Noah."[4] Hardly out of his vessel of refuge, "Noah built an altar to the Lord and offered burnt offerings on the altar . . . the Lord smelled the pleasing odor."[5] This is the very first time that something good comes from the earth! Rather than the stench of sin, a pleasant smell comes from Noah—whose name means pleasant. Remember the story of Cain. His sacrifice far from smelling good carried so much of the odor of death that God banished him. Now it smells good. God stays close by this altar. Ever after, every altar built for him, can become a place of encounter between human beings and himself.

And so when Abram builds an altar at Shechem, he sets in stone the appearance of the God who has just promised him a land

2. Gen 6:5.
3. Gen 6:7.
4. Gen 8:1.
5. Gen 8:20–21.

to inherit and a tribe to father.[6] Continuing his journey south to Bethel, he sets up another altar to mark the place where for the first time God he called out to God by name—the Lord. He will come back here later just before separating from his nephew Lot.[7] And when he settles more permanently in Hebron, yet another altar invites the presence of God.[8] And so Abraham, piles up his stones on top of each other. He's such a baby in faith. At Hebron God appears to him. God speaks to him. But on Mount Moriah the command of God will lead to a totally different experience. God does not ask him to build an altar but to offer his son Isaac as a sacrifice on one of these mountains.[9] Now a load of stones piled roughly on uneven ground is not good enough. For this sacrifice at once both supreme and aborted, it needed a whole mountain. It was a way for God to make it clear once and for all that when it came to sacrifices, burnt offerings and altars, he was in charge. For he says to Abraham: "The altar I will take care of. The sacrifice is my business—it's the ram caught by the horns in the bush close by."

Following the example of Abraham many of the patriarchs also built up their pile of stones: Isaac, Jacob and Moses. After God's miraculous intervention in delivering the victory over the Amalekites, Moses built an altar as a sign of gratitude and gave it the name Adonai-Nissi ("The Lord is my banner").[10] After Moses' experience on Mount Sinai, another altar reminds the Israelites that *this* God who speaks of heaven will, remarkably, speak to them here and now and bless them as long as they avoid all forms of idolatry.[11]

Altars are such an important sign of God's presence that sometimes they can unleash a war. When the sons of Reuben, the sons of Gad and the half-tribe of Manasseh settle on the other side

---

6. Gen 12:7.
7. Gen 13:4.
8. Gen 13:18.
9. Gen 22:20–21.
10. Exod 17:15–16.
11. Exod 20:22–26.

of the Jordan they build "an altar of great size"[12] close to the river. To many of the Israelites already installed in Canaan this would have appeared a move to a breakaway state for the true altar was in Siloam. They would have seen it as a breakaway state but maybe also as an act of idolatry. There was to be no altar other than Siloam. A detachment is sent in double-quick time from the other bank of the Jordan. War is threatening. Happily the Transjordanians reassure their brothers. It is not a question of an invasion but it is rather to honor and celebrate one and the same God. War is avoided . . . just. But this episode shows the limits and dangers inherent in building altars. Most of these altars were erected on the initiative of men who wanted to mark a personal encounter with their God. My altar against your altar. My experience against your experience. My God who shows himself to me here against yours who does not show himself at all, anywhere. My own form of worship against yours. All of this competitiveness is nothing less than a simple return to square one: Cain against Abel.

These small mounds with their cairns of stones existed for several thousand years but in the book of Exodus the presence of God would take another form.

---

12. Josh 22:10.

Itinerary 3

God Settles in the Midst of His People
The Sanctuary of the Desert

However you read the book of Exodus, the journey out of Egypt which culminates in the building of the sanctuary is a recent event, dating from approximately 1500–1250 BCE. In other words more water had flowed under the bridge of human history before this period than since. The time when there was no sanctuary was much longer than the period of its existence. This sanctuary lasted only as long as the Exodus—forty years at the most.

It is impossible to understand what is happening here without taking the trouble to come back to the exile in Egypt as it is described in the book of Exodus. Everything starts with a difficult economic situation. "The famine became severe throughout the world."[1] As in the time of the German occupation in Europe during World War II the boys in the family are sent to get fresh supplies to feed the family. Providentially the jealousy of Jacob's sons towards Joseph their brother turns into a blessing for the tribe. They find that their brother—now turned senior operator in Egypt—has an ear willing to listen to their pleas for ways of filling the refrigerator. But the bad times continue and the brief excursion to replenish supplies turns into a long stay in a foreign country. Better to live

1. Gen 41:57.

in the shadows of Joseph's palace than to return to the unforgiving land which theirs has become. Except that is that there is nothing so fragile as a political regime. The ephemeral nature of dynasties, royal families, and republics is often made starkly clear in the bare dates of their duration. A revolution stirs which ushers in one regime and another out, an open system to a closed system, from real freedoms to rights restricted at the whim of the powers that be. It only needed a new king who did not know Joseph for the situation to deteriorate badly. For immigrant populations suspicion turns easily to accusation and worse: jealousy, menial tasks, forced labor, impossible targets, genocide.

But God is neither deaf nor blind. "Then the Lord said: I have observed the misery of my people who are in Egypt; I have heard their cry on account of their taskmasters. Indeed, I know their sufferings, and I have come down to deliver them from the Egyptians, and to bring them up out of that land to a good and broad land, a land flowing with milk and honey."[2] Here begins the epic story of the exit from Egypt. The choice of Moses as supreme leader, not much of a talker and guilty of murder; the unrelenting stubborn obstinacy of the pharaoh who did not want to let go of this very cheap workforce; the death of all the Egyptian firstborns; a sea which was quite impossible to cross, as bitter to the taste as the waters of Mara, Merissa, and Meribah; the moaners who can only think of Egyptian meat; the smoking mountain, the shocking claps of thunder, the lightening, the sound of the trumpet and the fear that the voice of God will destroy absolutely everything. And finally amidst all this drama who says plainly that he wishes to live in their midst. What a ridiculous idea!

It's the obsession of a God who cannot and will not live alone in splendid isolation. It's true that he frequently came to meet men but it was always rather a brief stay. And there are no altars scattered hither and yon to satisfy or pacify him. He wants none of it. With the birth of this people whom he brought out of Egypt, the time is ripe, he thinks, for a change of plan: "Human beings can no longer live in my home so I am going to live with them!"

2. Exod 3:7–8.

And so there is a twist in the story and what twist could be more important? So who are they, these people with whom God wishes to cohabit?

430 years in Egypt

From 2015, go back 430 years to 1585. In England, Elizabeth the First is on the throne. Between the reigns of Elizabeth I and Elizabeth II is a very long time! It was a very long time for the Israelites as they slaved away for nothing. Four hundred thirty years in which even births were controlled. Four hundred thirty years of hopelessness in which the slightest attempt at revolt is severely put down. Four hundred thirty years in which to lose touch with your roots. Four hundred thirty years of prayers without a single reply. Do they have a sense of being a people loved by God? Undoubtedly not. Even from the moment that they leave Egypt the sense of their national identity is probably very weak, not to say nonexistent, given that "a mixed crowd also went up with them."[3] When all is said and done they were a group which barely held together, made of some from here and others from there.

Spiritually, their stay in worldly Egypt has removed any sign of the practice of the religion of their fathers. Don't imagine that they began their journey with a few words from the Holy Scriptures (which did not exist then anyway). Don't imagine that they were able to erect an unauthorized altar here and there by the wayside so as to offer an offering or a sacrifice. Don't imagine them opening Sabbath together on Friday evening. None of that because slavery had swept all of that away. Even Moses their future leader, appears not to know exactly the identity of this God who is calling him.[4]

Four hundred thirty years building in Egypt, and not only towns but palaces and temples, for it is common knowledge—it is always the case—that one needs cheap labor to achieve grand

3. Exod 12:38.
4. Exod 3:13.

designs. Two of the grandest sites in Egypt were built during the captivity of the Israelites. Thus it is that the truly fabulous complex at Karnak whose construction began under Sestoris I in 1971 BCE has lasted two thousand years; so also the funeral temple of Del El Bahari, begun in the eleventh dynasty by Montouhotep (2061–2010). These places and many others are of breathtaking dimensions. The enormous columns are liberally distributed. Frescoes, obelisks and statues vie with each other in beauty. Even today after the passage of time the colors are stunning. This was the sort of world in which the Israelites lived even if they were not involved in the construction of these particular sites. So then when they leave Egypt they have the bulging muscles owned by all the masons in the world; yes and calluses. And what is more, I have no doubt that they carry in their minds the many Egyptian religious ceremonies, the parade of the sun barge on the Nile, the funeral processions. Did they merely witness these practices or did they participate? It would be comforting to think they simply saw such things as they went about their duties. But what happened in the wilderness, after the long absence of Moses when he went up the mountain to meet with God, sadly points to the second option. The words "come, make gods for us, who shall go before us"[5] reminds very sharply of an Egyptian procession behind an animal divinity. This is probably not a people spiritually pure, innocent, and naive who are leaving Egypt. God has a "holy" job on his hands. Moses too!

The Tent of Meeting

Any careful reader of the book of Exodus will have noticed it: this book repeats itself. As far as the sanctuary is concerned chapters 25–31 tell how it should be built and how it should operate. But the episode of the golden calf interrupts the narrative flow.[6] Once they are forgiven, the covenant is renewed.[7] The construction is

5. Exod 32:1.
6. Exod 32.
7. Exod 34:10–28.

again described in detail as if it was necessary to start again from the very beginning.⁸ Between the two descriptive sections lies a short paragraph which often goes unnoticed. However it is worth pausing to look at it:

> Now Moses used to take the tent and pitch it outside the camp, far off from the camp; he called it the tent of meeting. And everyone who sought the Lord would go out to the tent of meeting, which was outside the camp. Whenever Moses went out to the tent, all the people would rise and stand, each of them, at the entrance of their tents and watch Moses until he had gone into the tent. When Moses entered the tent, the pillar of cloud would descend and stand at the entrance of the tent, and the Lord would speak with Moses. When all the people saw the pillar of cloud standing at the entrance of the tent, all the people would rise and bow down, all of them, at the entrance of their tent. Thus the Lord used to speak to Moses face to face, as one speaks to a friend. Then he would return to the camp; but his young assistant, Joshua son of Nun, would not leave the tent.⁹

This tent (*moed*) erected by Moses does not carry the same name as the dwelling (*miqdash*) mentioned in Exodus 25:8. And what is more it is not situated in the same place. The dwelling in chapter 25 is clearly placed at the center of the encampment. This tent of meeting is on the outside. As its name indicates, it is the place where God comes to speak to Moses, face to face, as a man would speak to a friend. Why this type of text which speaks about God coming to visit his friend Moses is overlooked in favor of those which say that you cannot see God and live?¹⁰ It would be a shame to smooth over the rough edges of the book of Exodus. Every tension in the biblical text (and there are many) must make one think. You might explain it this way: after the regrettable episode of the golden calf, Moses fears that in spite of God's pardon and the renewing of the covenant, the people become nervous about a God

---

8. Exod 35:30—40:38.
9. Exod 33:7-11.
10. Exod 33:20.

who lives in the middle of the camp, after they have put themselves beyond the pale and are no longer worthy of his presence—and besides it could be threatening. Moses then plants the tent outside the camp. It is not the house of God but it is his lodgings, shall we say, where he agrees to meet them. This is exactly the explanation given in the Septuagint, the Greek translation of the Old Testament used by the apostles and the early church. "And Moses took his tent and set it outside the camp, far away."[11] The book of Exodus shows us a little of the human reticence towards the outrageous project of the God who comes to live right in the middle of his people. "Lord it is disturbing if you come to live in the middle of the camp. Stay outside, it's better that way." The modern version of such an episode goes like this: build religious houses where one can meet God, generally speaking once a week, for two or three hours at the most, rather than letting him in among us. "No one wants a squatter-God in their place."

The Construction of the Sanctuary

Two verses order the building of the sanctuary: "Have them make me a sanctuary, so that I may dwell among them. In accordance with all that I show you concerning the pattern of the tabernacle and of all its furniture, so you shall make it."[12] And: "See that you make them according to the pattern for them, which is being shown you on the mountain."[13]

The structure of these verses is simple. There's no need of theological gymnastics to understand them but this does not do away with the need for a rigorous reading. Two important ideas need to be separated.

---

11. Exod 33:7 (LXX).
12. Exod 25:8–9.
13. Exod 25:40.

Everything Must Be Done according to the Model

Why is the building of the temple of Karnak spread out over two thousand years? Simply because each new pharaoh on coming to power thought the temple left by his predecessor too small, not broad enough, not high enough, that the blue was too dark, the columns too thin. In other words each wanted to leave his own mark on the building. Constant expansions and refurbishments according to the whim of the prince. But for the house of God there is to be nothing of the sort. If it is his house then he will decide on the plan, the furnishings, and the decoration. Nothing is left to human initiative, not to the imagination of the architect, not to the tastes of the planning committee, not to the alleged talents of Mr. X and Mrs. Y who of course know all there is to know when it comes to religious buildings.

Everything then is shown, told and repeated twice to Moses in the greatest detail.[14] Dimensions, building materials, decoration. Here for example is the note on the seven-branched candlestick commonly called the lampstand:[15]

- Hammered out of pure gold;
- Foot, stem, cups, buttons and flowers from one single piece;
- Six branches coming out from its sides, three from one and three from the other;
- Three cups shaped like almond flowers with buds and flowers on each of the two branches;
- On the lampstands four cups in the shape of an almond with buds and flowers;
- One bud under its two first branches;
- One bud under the next two branches and the same for the other branches;

---

14. Exod 33:30—40:38.
15. Exod 25:31–38.

- Buds and branches made in a single piece, in pure hammered (burnished) gold;
- Seven lamps which light the space in front of it;
- Wick trimmers and trays of pure gold;
- Total weight of the gold needed for producing the lampstands: thirty kilos of pure gold.

You can imagine that when God first said that he wanted a sanctuary to be built for him quite a number of volunteers showed up for work. "Build a sanctuary, yes we know how to do that. We made several in Egypt, big ones too." Masons, plasterers, decorators, sculptors, all gifted with the skills passed from father to son over four hundred thirty years. All of them wanting to do something for this God who had delivered them out of slavery. They would not even have discussed their wages. At least on this desert building site there would be no slave driver eager to crack the whip. At least there would be no terrible work rates. And building the house of God on earth has got to be better than building temples for cat-gods, rams, jackals, hippopotamus, ibis, beetle or a vulture.

You can imagine the astonishment when Moses brought out the plans. Everything was in black and white in the greatest detail. No never-ending site meeting or different trades trying to make the architect see sense. Nothing other to do than follow the plan. And they followed it to the letter. So that in the last two chapters of the book of Exodus the expression "as the Lord had commanded Moses" is a refrain which appears fifteen times, several times in the same verses: "The Israelites had done all of the work just as the Lord had commanded Moses. When Moses saw that they had done all the work just as the Lord had commanded, he blessed them."[16] One thing is certain: the plan provided by God and trusted to Moses was scrupulously followed.

---

16. Exod 39:42–43.

The Nature of the Model

The word for model (*tabnith*) can be misleading. It simply belongs to normal building language—the word uses the root of the verb "to build." Thus, much later, David will give to Solomon the *tabnith* for the temple, that is the plan.[17] There is no reason to think other than that the model shown to Moses was a mock-up which had to become a reality. This model is not described as coming down form heaven, which makes it a very different experience from that of John in Revelation where he sees the Holy City descending from heaven.[18] Moses is summoned to the mountain where God shows him exactly what he wants.

A Sanctuary Similar to . . . but Different from . . .

The workers would no doubt have been surprised by the meticulous precision of the plan. Would they have been similarly surprised by the general look of the building? Not really. For they quickly found in the master plan for the building something familiar: an outer court, a holy place, and a most holy place. Three sections. All Egyptian temples were built in the same way. Anywhere in the world, every temple and every sanctuary ever built was the same. Even some famous palaces have this threefold division with the sovereign, regarded as a god, living in the third section inaccessible to mere mortals.[19] But as for the rest everything is different.

The size for one thing. The enclosure of the sanctuary measured approximately forty-five meters long by twenty-two meters wide. The house itself (the holy and most holy place) measured fifteen meters by five meters. This is a long way away from the great temple of Amon at Karnak: two thousand four hundred meters in circumference. Its hypostyle room and its one hundred thirty-four columns measure one hundred meters wide and fifty-five meters high. To use another comparison, St. Peter's Basilica in Rome

---

17. 1 Chron 28:11.
18. Rev 21:2.
19. See, e.g., the palace of Ottoman sultans in Istanbul (Topkapi).

could accommodate five whole sanctuaries in its length and three in its width.

Next the positioning. Compared to Egyptian temples the sanctuary is back to front. The entrance is on the eastern side. The sun is at one's back when you come to worship first thing in the morning. It is going down for the evening offering. You never face this heavenly body because the sun is not a god which you worship.

This sanctuary does not contain any likenesses of animals because the people knew only too well the beasts of the Egyptian religion. At most they will use the skins of goats and rams and for the coverings. Animal skins, nothing more.

And this sanctuary is portable. The circumstances absolutely require that. But there is more. God does not ask them to build him a house where they come to visit him in one place. The God of the Bible pitches his tent wherever there are any human beings.

Last, this sanctuary carries no inscriptions. There is nothing to read. No mention of the founding pharaoh, or the architect, or the site director, or the pharaoh's wife, or her hairdresser, or the firstborn son, or the idolized princess or the favorite priest. Not even the name of Moses.

Compared to Egypt, God works with simplicity to say the very least. He also has lessons to teach. It will not take years and years to put up this fragile structure (not a single stone column but just some wooden rods). All those who are involved in building it and all those who watch it being put up, are students in the University of the Wilderness. For this building is above all designed to deconstruct the beliefs, traditions, habits and customs of Egypt. In some strange way, it is Egypt that makes the sanctuary of the Exodus what it is. In other words, this sanctuary is a response to the stay in Egypt, a labor of reconstruction and purification both intellectual and spiritual. It's all very simple compared with the hotchpotch of Egyptian religion. The construction was simplified and so was the message it conveyed. It is a theological construction for it tells all the Israelites who is this God who brought them out of Egypt. It matters more to God to live in the midst of his people than to have a designated sacred space. This is a God who cohabits with human beings.

ITINERARY 4

The Symbolism of the Sanctuary

AS WE APPROACH THIS rather more demanding chapter it is important to avoid three pitfalls: ethnocentrism, an atomistic reading of the text, and a Christian reading of it.

The first pitfall is ethnocentrism: the tendency to consider the sanctuary in the Bible as the first and only sanctuary, the reference point according by which all else must be interpreted. There were hundreds of sanctuaries, temples and other sacred spaces before this one all following the same model. The sanctuary is not invented in the book of Exodus or anywhere else in the Bible. By comparing this sanctuary with others we can better understand its significance. As is always the case, there are differences which explode with meaning especially when the texts diverge from each other.

The second pitfall is atomistic reading, the tendency to put biblical texts under the microscope and find a meaning in absolutely everything. That is not to say that a superficial reading is adequate. Never. There is too much negligence, even carelessness and superficiality in our reading of the Bible. While our tables may groan under the weight of good food, the famine that Amos warned us about becomes more of a threat. When it comes to the sanctuary I do not believe that we should or could find an explanation for everything. I am thinking particularly of all the details that abound in the description of all the pieces of sacred furniture. To take only one example, the lampstand, I do not think it is necessary to find an explanation for the four cups made in the shape of an almond. Consult your concordance, worse still, your computer to discover the possible biblical texts which would explain the role of the almond, or the symbolism of the number four and you risk stumbling on interpretations which are often not simply unverifiable but patently absurd. When the text goes into such a depth of detail it is first and foremost to tell the craftsmen in charge of making the specified piece that they have room to invent nothing but must follow scrupulously the plan produced by God. It is also to indicate the difference from the Egyptian temples. In the sanctuary the ornamentation was inanimate. It is much less risky, too: Egypt knew nothing of almond worship! And last, it is to test the faithfulness of the craftsmen. A vague and blurred plan could give rise to all sorts of interpretations. A definite plan requires obedience.

The third pitfall is a Christian reading of the text, the tendency to read these texts as if we were the only intended readers. These texts, indeed all the texts in the Bible, were not written primarily with us in mind. They do not belong to us really. We read them, to use a well-known phrase, standing on the shoulders of the intended recipients. The Old Testament belongs to the Jews. It is their inheritance. It is a bit of a cheek for some Christians to tell the Jews how they should interpret their own texts. Same thing for the New Testament. The Letter to the Romans is addressed to the Romans in the first instance. But with all these texts the complex process of canonization gives us a particular license. It is true that they do not belong to us, but we can, we must read them for other people's stories can certainly be a source of inspiration and reflection for us as well. It is an invitation to read, an opportunity to be inspired but not a right to looting and pillaging. So to the lampstand again: it is not because it gives light that I am entitled to conclude that it symbolizes first and foremost Jesus of Nazareth, the light of the world. The real explanation may lie somewhere else, as we shall soon see.

A Split Universe

The religions of Mesopotamia, Iran, the Indian subcontinent, and central Asia as well as Israel have at least one thing in common which is also found in the philosophy of Plato: belief in a split universe. So the mountains, the towns, the sanctuaries and the temples, in fact the whole earth, correspond to certain heavenly "ideals" or realities. Any sacred space on earth is merely the shadow of a holy temple. Every city is but a copy of a heavenly city. In the heavens there is a Nineveh, a Babylon, indeed a Jerusalem, the real thing, an archetype for what exists on earth. Even Plato's ideal Republic which he acknowledges does not exist on earth, exists in the heavens.[1]

Mircea Eliade, the great phenomenologist of religions, sums this view up well: "The world that surrounds us, then, the world in which the presence and the work of man are felt—the mountains that he climbs, populated and cultivated regions, navigable rivers, cities, sanctuaries—all these have an extraterrestrial archetype, be it conceived as a plan, as a form, or purely and simply as a 'double' existing on a higher cosmic level."[2]

The Heavenly Temple in the Bible

It is undoubtedly the case that the editors of the Bible—of Exodus and all the other books—were aware of this split cosmology, this general understanding of the world, which was virtually universal. However, if we take a closer look we can see that the list of texts referring unmistakably to the existence of a heavenly sanctuary or temple is pretty short.

In the Old Testament, it comes down to poetical texts. Now Hebrew poetry operates according to some clear conventions, especially parallelism. Psalm 11 says this:

---

1. Plato, *Republic*, 592b.
2. Eliade, *Cosmos and History*, 9.

> The Lord is in his holy temple;
> the Lord's throne is in heaven.
> His eyes behold, his gaze examines humankind.[3]

These three lines must be read as a whole, the second repeating and explaining the first. So what is this about? The place where God resides. The first line is not enough. The two fragments must be read together. The expression "holy temple" is explained by "throne in heaven." From this psalm we are entirely justified in thinking that the Lord's holy temple is his throne.

Another poetic passage about the holy temple conveys another message:

> In my distress I called upon the Lord;
> to my God I cried for help.
> From his temple he heard my voice,
> and my cry to him reached his ears.[4]

It's another parallelism, between the place (temple) and the ability of the Lord to listen. The words "temple of God" conveys the idea of a God who listens and comes to our aid. This same psalm can also be found in 2 Samuel. Two other texts can also be thrown into the mix:

> But the Lord is in his holy temple;
> let all the earth keep silence before him![5]

> Hear, you peoples, all of you;
> listen, O earth, and all that is in it;
> and let the Lord God be a witness against you,
> the Lord from his holy temple.[6]

Generally speaking, the Old Testament is quite limited in its references to the heavenly sanctuary/temple. The New Testament is on the same line except for the book of Revelation and the so-called

---

3. Ps 11:4.
4. Ps 18:6.
5. Hab 2:20.
6. Mic 1:2.

Epistle to the Hebrews. We will come back to each of them in two separate chapters.[7] It suffices to say, for the moment, that biblical authors are rather cautious, discrete and moderate whenever they refer to a heavenly temple or sanctuary. Actually, the authors of the Bible had to swim against the tide in order to maintain this view. For in all the extra-biblical literature, often apocalyptic in nature, the references to a heavenly sanctuary/temple are numerous.

Before considering the most significant among them, we must be clear on an issue of methodology. There is a vast area called the Second Temple literature which covers the period 515 BCE–70 CE. In this category we place not only the apocryphal books but the Pseudepigrapha, the Qumran texts, the works of Philo of Alexandria and Flavius Josephus. Sometimes the rabbinic literature (the Midrash, the Pesharim, the Targumim) is also included even if it comes from a later period. There is no question of granting any of these texts the same status of canonical books. But when today one wants to keep abreast of events one has to read the newspapers, listen to the radio and/or look at televised reports, because it is impossible to be there. When you read a newspaper, you do not ask whether the journalist is inspired. You use your intelligence to learn and to understand. It is in this spirit that we can consult this extra-biblical literature. Not to be inspired by them but to know and to understand by means of them.

Sanctuaries and Temples, from before the Creation of the World

What is clear from the Second Temple literature is that the city of Jerusalem and its temple predate the creation of the world. Here is the opening of the inaugural prayer for the temple, as put on the lips of King Solomon in the book of Wisdom:

> You have chosen me to be king of your people
> and to be judge over your sons and daughters.

---

7. See below, part 2, itineraries 4 and 6.

You have given command to build a temple on your holy mountain,
and an altar in the city of your habitation,
a copy of the holy tent that you prepared from the beginning.[8]

The second book of Baruch is even more explicit about the preexistence of the city and the temple:

And the Lord said to me:
"This city shall be delivered up for a time,
And the people shall be chastened for a time,
And the world will not be forgotten.

Or do you think that this is the city of which I said: *On the palms of my hands I have carved you?* It is not this building that is in your midst now; it is that which will be revealed, with me, that was already prepared from the moment that I decided to create Paradise. And I showed it to Adam before he sinned. But when he transgressed the commandment, it was taken away from him—as also Paradise. After these thinks, I showed it to my servant Abraham in the night between the portions of the victims. And again I showed it also to Moses on Mount Sinai when I showed him the likeness of the tabernacle and all its vessels. Behold, now it is preserved with me—as also Paradise. Now go away and do as I command you."[9]

Not only do the city and the temple already exist but they are described as being the nerve center. So, for example, in the first book of Enoch, the angels Michael, Surafel, and Gabriel "looked down from the heavenly sanctuary and saw much blood being shed upon the earth, and all lawlessness being wrought upon the earth."[10] Elsewhere it is Enoch, taken to heaven without anyone knowing where he is, who is sent to speak to the fallen angels (known as the watchmen) "who have abandoned the high heaven, the holy eternal place, and have defiled themselves with women, as

---

8. Wis 9:7–8.
9. *2 Bar.* 4:1–7.
10. *1 En.* 9:1.

their deeds move the children of the world, and have taken unto themselves wives."[11]

The sanctuary in the heavens is also a theater for liturgy. A service of worship to the Lord takes place there mainly conducted by the angels. The document called *Songs for the Sabbath Sacrifice*, found in cave 4 at Qumran, shows this as do several others. These are songs and praises celebrating the arrival of the Sabbath. The point of this text is to convince the faithful here below that his worship has an equivalent in heaven: what man does on earth corresponds to what the angels do in heaven. The book of Ezekiel serves as a reference point for this, particularly the first ten chapters which describe the throne of God and its chariots, and chapter 40 which paints a picture of a temple in the heavens. In this Qumran text, the formulae used to describe the sanctuary in heaven are extravagant and repeated: "princes in his sanctuary," "wise embellishments to the holy of holies," "noble place," "chariots in his sanctuary," "divine temple," "holiness of his inner sanctuary."[12] The degree of emphasis surely tells us something important. The sanctuary/temple in heaven seems to correspond to much more than a piece of architecture however huge the size of it may be.

The Universe—That's the Real Temple

Two Jewish authors help us to understand the symbolism of sacred space: Philo of Alexandria and Flavius Josephus. They have described it in their own way and without adding anything to the traditions of their fathers.

Philo was born around 15–10 BCE to a rich Jewish family that had settled in Alexandria, the main Jewish colony of the Mediterranean basin. He received a high-quality education. His mind wrestled with the ideas of great philosophers—Greeks, Stoics, Pythagoreans and Aristotelians. As one who was very attached to his Jewish roots he had no doubt that the law of Moses was superior

11. *1 En.* 12:4.
12. 4Q403.

to the whole apparatus of Greek law. Philo was convinced that the sacred text had a deep meaning hidden below the surface of its literal meaning. He inhabits the margins of theology and philosophy.

Flavius Josephus was born in Jerusalem in 37 CE. Though he was from the tribe of Levi he nevertheless was a Roman citizen. His work has taken on a considerable historical significance. Without his writings we would know virtually nothing of the history of Judea between 100 BCE and the end of the first Jewish rebellion in 74 CE. What is important for our purpose is that Philo and Josephus tell the same story about the temple in spite of the fact that they come from two entirely different backgrounds. Their view is easily captured: the temple is the universe. Philo writes:

> Moreover, he [God] chose the materials of this embroidery, selecting with great care what was most excellent out of an infinite quantity, choosing materials equal in number to the elements of which the world was made, and having a direct relation to them; the elements being the earth and the water, and the air and the fire. For the fine flax is produced from the earth, and the purple from the water, and the hyacinth color is compared to the air (for, by nature, it is black), and the scarlet is likened to fire, because each is of a red color; for it followed of necessity that those who were preparing a temple made by hands for the Father and Ruler of the universe must take essences similar to those of which he made the universe itself.[13]

On the same line of thought, Josephus writes:

> Now here one may wonder at the ill will which men bear to us, and which they profess to bear on account of our despising that Deity which they pretend to honor; for if anyone do but consider the fabric of the tabernacle, and take a view of the garments of the high priest, and of those vessels which we make use of in our sacred ministration, he will find that our legislator was a divine man, and that we are unjustly reproached by others: for if anyone do without prejudice, and with judgment, look

---

13. Philo, *Moses*, 2:88.

upon these things, he will find they were every one made in way of imitation and representation of the universe.[14]

Such views are surprising and one wonders whether they were shared by the Israelites or were quite simply the creation of minds in search of something novel or even sensational. But these views are also found in the rabbinic literature as seen in this Midrash on the book of Genesis:

> THIS IS NONE OTHER THAN THE HOUSE OF GOD, AND THIS IS THE GATE OF HEAVEN (XXVIII, 17). R. Aha said: [God assured him]: "This gate will be opened for many righteous men like thyself." R. Simeon b. Yohai said: The celestial temple is higher than the terrestrial one only by eighteen miles. What is the proof? WEZEH (AND THIS IS) THE GATE OF HEAVEN, eighteen being the numerical value of WEZEH.[15]

The New Testament itself echoes this belief. The disciples were marked by this tradition. When Jesus announces the destruction of the temple where no stone will remain on another, they are in a state of shock. So they ask the Lord for further clarification for the destruction of the temple of which he speaks cannot refer to the end of the world: "Tell us, when will this be, and what will be the sign of your coming and of the end of the age?"[16] The disciples' reaction is perfectly in line with the descriptions of Philo and Josephus: the temple is the world. If the temple is destroyed that means that the world will suffer the same fate at the same time.

Neither Philo nor Josephus satisfies himself with a general account. They both enter into detail and provide what one might call a cosmic view of the temple. Every piece of holy furniture is explained in relation to the universe. Hence:

---

14. Josephus, *Ant.* 3.179–80.
15. *Gen. Rab.* 69:7.
16. Matt 24:3.

The Candlestick

> The Creator therefore, wishing that there should be a model upon earth among us of the seven-lighted sphere as it exists in heaven, explained this exquisite work to be made, namely, this candlestick.[17]

The Table of Breads

According to Philo:

> And loaves are placed on the seventh day on the sacred table, being equal in number to the months of the year, twelve loaves, arranged in two rows of six each, in accordance with the arrangement of the equinoxes; for there are two equinoxes every year, the vernal and the autumnal, which are each reckoned by periods of six months.[18]

According to Josephus:

> And when he ordered twelve loaves to be set on the table, he denoted the year, as distinguished into so many months.[19]

The High Priest's Vestments

According to Philo:

> But the high priest is commanded to wear a similar dress when he goes into the holy of holies to offer incense, because linen is not made of any animal that dies, as woolen garments are. He is also commanded to wear another robe also, having very beautiful embroidery and

---

17. Philo, *Heir*, :225.
18. Philo, *Spec. Laws*, 1:172.
19. Josephus, *Ant.* 3.182.

ornament upon it, so that it may seem to be a copy and representation of the world.[20]

According to Josephus:

> Now the vestment of the high priest being made of linen, signified the earth; the blue denoted the sky, being like lightning in its pomegranates, and in the noise of the bells resembling thunder. And for the ephod, it showed that God had made the universe of four [elements].[21]

The Three-Part Sanctuary/Temple

Josephus explains the correspondence between the different parts of the universe and the sanctuary:

> When Moses distinguished the tabernacle into three parts, and allowed two of them to the priests, as a place accessible and common, he denoted the land and the sea, these being of general access to all; but he set apart the third division for God, because heaven is inaccessible to men.[22]

What is found in Philo and Josephus correspond to the prevalent views of the age: with the Israelites as with all of the ancient Near East there could be no universe without a temple. Without the temple/sanctuary the world is without form and void as it was before the act of creation. The universe is not subdued but hostile. That is why the desert regions are likened to chaos. When anyone thinks about living in such places it is vital to build as soon as possible as temple/sanctuary that will transform them into habitable places under the authority of God. That is the reason also for the building of the sanctuary in the wilderness. It was not possible to live in a place where God was absent. The continued presence of God in the cloud pervading the sanctuary reassures the people. The

---

20. Philo, *Spec. Laws*, 1:84.
21. Josephus, *Ant.* 3.184.
22. Josephus, *Ant.* 3.181.

place in which they must live is part of the universe because God is present there. What is under normal circumstances hostile and inhospitable terrain becomes a place where they can live: the water is pure, food is provided regularly, the wild animals are tamed. If at any time God was banished from this space—which would be any form of idolatry—then nature would lapse into chaos here below. It is a piece of cosmological symbolism but just as importantly an existential lesson: God in the middle of the universe, God in the midst of his people. But more than that it is a case of human beings right at the center of the world. What goes for the wilderness applies also to any capital city. Without a temple it does not from part of the universe. You can understand why—since the conquest of Jerusalem signaled by the building of his palace David did not rest until he had built a temple there as well. We also understand that a real capital city is not built merely around a temple but like a temple, as it were the navel of the world. A new kingdom cannot be imagined without the construction or restoration of the temple and of the city which embraces it. It is in this spirit that we must read the extraordinary description of the New Jerusalem in the book of Revelation, a city with a new temple and indeed the city of a new world, as big as a whole continent with each side measuring a full two thousand five hundred kilometers!

A symbol of the universe, the center of the world, the sign of the presence of God. But how does a sanctuary/temple actually work? What goes on there?

Itinerary 5

The God Who Eats with His Own
or, Sacrifices in the Old Testament

> Sacrifice. A word which, for most people, evokes rituals both exotic and barbaric, terrible carnage, altars running with the blood of victims whose throats had been cut and who had been dismembered, huge and absurd pyres on which hard-won riches are destroyed and wasted and precious food with it. And inevitably there arises in the mind a picture of these primitive religions with their voracious and cruel divinities, and fearful idols who must be bribed with food offerings and whose anger must be endlessly appeased, never satisfied, thirsty for blood, enjoying the spectacle of those being put to death and of all this destruction by which the faithful think that they can recommend themselves to their tyrant lords.[1]

THERE ARE SO MANY reasons for me to hate the word sacrifice. However since we are talking about the sanctuary and the temple we can hardly get away from it. For having gone through the veil or the entry point into the enclosure there is no way of avoiding the sacrificial altar. Made out of acacia wood, this square measured two-meters-fifty long and one-meter-fifty high. But in the temple

---

1. Grappe and Marx, *Le sacrifice*, 9 (translation mine).

of Solomon the proportions were grander: made out of bronze, the altar measured ten meters square by five high. Facing the altar we are inevitably at the heart of the covenant between God and Israel. Sacrifice is at the very center of the Old Testament. The angles of the sacrificial table are sharp and could easily cut into your skin. God has not rounded the edges. But what exactly was he trying to say?

In the Old Testament no less than fifty oracles mention sacrifices; twenty psalms, proverbs or wisdom texts; more than sixty stories. The only books not to mention sacrifices are Obadiah, Nahum, Haggai, Ruth, the Song of Solomon, Lamentations and Esther.

The book of Leviticus, which regulates the sacrificial system, makes neither pleasant nor easy reading. It certainly does not make it to the top of the charts for readers of the Bible. It is certain that they will not begin with it. We often have a tendency to give prominence to legal texts. We give the impression that the Israelites focused on these norms and regulations. Do we today in our everyday lives find something riveting in the criminal statutes or in civil law? Would historians or sociologists who wanted to describe any society in the twenty-first century naturally turn to such types of texts to paint a picture of any country? Probably not. First because there are many laws which are never enforced. Then because it is not the letter of the law which creates justice but its interpretation. Thus we must turn towards the stories which feature an actual sacrifice rather than the maze of dry, technical pronouncements where we can easily get lost. And so an important word of clarification before proceeding: this chapter is not intended to address every aspect of sacrifice, but simply what I consider the fundamental principle in the light of which everything else must be understood.

The Babylonians, Assyrians, Hittites, Phoenicians and Carthaginians, to mention only a few practiced the sorts of sacrifice found in the Bible long before the Israelites. There are no great innovations in the Old Testament. Again a comparative approach can aid us in our understanding. Here, for example, is a text which tells the story of the Carthaginian army. In 310 BCE it undergoes a terrible defeat, after constant assaults by the army from Syracuse led by Agathocle. Here in the words of Diodore of Sicily is how the Carthaginians react to this military disaster:

> Therefore the Carthaginians, believing that the misfortune had come to them from the gods, betook themselves to every manner of supplication of the divine powers; and, because they believed that Heracles, who was worshipped in their mother city, was exceedingly angry with them, they sent a large sum of money and many of the most expensive offerings to Tyre. Since they had come as colonists from that city, it had been their custom in the earlier period to send to the god a tenth of all that was paid into the public revenue; but later, when they had acquired great wealth and were receiving more considerable revenues, they sent very little indeed, holding the divinity of little account. But turning to repentance because of this misfortune, they bethought them of all the gods of Tyre. They even sent from their temples in supplication the golden shrines with their images, believing that they would better appease the wrath of the god if the offerings were sent for the sake of winning forgiveness. They also alleged that Cronus had turned against them inasmuch as in former times they had been accustomed to sacrifice to this god the noblest of their sons, but more recently, secretly buying and nurturing children, they had sent these to the sacrifice; and when an investigation was made, some of those who had been sacrificed were discovered to have been suppositious. When they had given thought to these things and saw their enemy encamped before their walls, they were filled with superstitious dread, for they believed that they had neglected the honours of the gods that had been established by their fathers. In their zeal to make amends for their omission, they selected two hundred of the noblest children and sacrificed them publicly; and others who were under suspicion sacrificed themselves voluntarily, in number not less than three hundred.[2]

This story is very enlightening. It shows the natural response of the soul in all religions beyond the Bible. Here the military

---

2. Diodorus Siculus, *Library of History*, XX:14.

debacle is attributed to the gods—in other examples sickness or any natural disaster has the very same cause. Left to themselves the Israelites would have probably done the same. The Carthaginians, as elsewhere, tried to appease the wrath of the divinity by reinstating some more radical practices. They had got out of the habit of sacrificing the children of the richest and most powerful families. They had substituted second-class sacrifices, children raised from birth specifically to be sacrificed. So they came back to the traditional practice and five hundred children lost their lives.

When it came to the practice of sacrifices, the Israelites were called by God to stand out, to be different even if that was not always easy with such strong forces of paganism surrounding them. For the Israelites:

- There is no offering of sacrifices before embarking on a war, to guarantee victory through divine grace, or to regroup after a defeat, but they eliminated the guilty person or selected only a limited number of soldiers;[3]
- There is no offering of sacrifices so that a sterile woman could become fertile, but they prayed as did Hannah, mother of Samuel;[4]
- There is no offering of sacrifices in order to ensure a good harvest but they offered to the Lord the first sheaf after the harvest time as a sign of gratitude;[5]
- There is no offering of sacrifices to bring healing from sickness, but rather bathing seven times in the Jordan was the cure for leprosy;[6]
- There is no offering of sacrifices to bring forgiveness for their errors but they had to confess their sin.[7]

---

3. Cf. Judg 7 for the story of Gidion and Josh 7 for the story of Achan.
4. 1 Sam 1:9.
5. Cf. Lev 23:9 and the offering of first fruits.
6. Cf. 2 Kgs 5 and the healing of Naaman.
7. Job's friends never asked him to offer a sacrifice. Rather, they advised him to find out what sin provoked God's wrath.

Just as the sanctuary in the desert deconstructed Egyptian beliefs so the sacrificial system in the Old Testament deconstructed the prevailing practices. When it comes to sacrifices for sin where non-biblical religions called for sacrifices (plural), God shows clearly his preference for the singular: one sin, one sacrifice and only one. To the Carthaginians and all those who practiced human sacrifice, God said: "Do not lay a hand on the boy."[8] God also said that the firstborns belonged to him and must not be proffered to him.[9] God further insisted that it was not so much what you offered but the spirit in which you offered it. He says to Cain: "First fix the problem with your brother before bringing your offering."[10] God also says: "There is no catalogue of sins, ranging from the most serious to the most trivial with a corresponding tariff of sacrifices. What you have to offer is not set by the seriousness of your offense but by your social rank and wealth."[11] God says: "Blood yes, but not only." "If you cannot afford two turtledoves or two pigeons, you shall bring as your offering for the sin that you have committed one-tenth of an ephah of choice flour for a sin offering."[12] In other words God says this: "I am the only one able to cover your nakedness. It's me, and only me, you can provide the ram caught in a thicket by its horns."[13] In others words, God says this: "Never imagine that your sacrifice, whatever it is, gives you discharge from your sin. Never forget that I am the only one who can fix the problem."

This lesson should have been heard. It was not the case. See the details of the great carnage when the temple was inaugurated by King Solomon:

> Solomon offered as sacrifices of well being to the Lord twenty-two thousand oxen and one hundred twenty thousand sheep. So the king and all the people of Israel

8. Gen 22:12.
9. Exod 13:11–16.
10. Gen 4:1–7.
11. See Lev 4 and 5.
12. Lev 5:11.
13. Gen 22:13–14.

dedicated the house of the Lord. The same day the king consecrated the middle of the court that was in front of the house of the Lord; for there he offered the burnt offerings and the grain offerings and the fat pieces of the sacrifices of well-being, because the bronze altar that was before the Lord was too small to receive the burnt offerings and the grain offerings and the fat pieces of the sacrifices of well-being.[14]

Vegetarians, defenders of animal rights, and all other sensitive souls, this is not for you. A hundred sacrifices a minute more or less. Who else would be satisfied with such practices? What can be said about the behavior of a certain Manasseh, king of Judah, for fifty-five years? "For he rebuilt the high places that his father Hezekiah had destroyed; he erected altars for Baal, made a sacred pole, as King Ahab of Israel had done, worshiped all the host of heaven, and served them. He built altars in the house of the Lord, of which the Lord had said, 'In Jerusalem I will put my name.' He built altars for all the host of heaven in the two courts of the house of the Lord."[15] Or even more: what shall we say about the human beings sacrificed by Manasseh himself who took his own son to the fire, just like his colleague Achaz, king of Judah,[16] or the Sepharvaites.[17] It did not take the prophets very long to react and to raise their voices to God against such sinister perversions.

Stop the Carnage!

The old prophet Samuel had already warned King Saul who was seeking to excuse his own disobedience on the basis that his looting of livestock large and small was really to present sacrifices to the Lord.

---

14. 1 Kgs 8: 63–64.
15. 2 Kgs 21:3–5.
16. 2 Kgs 16:3.
17. 2 Kgs 17:31.

> Has the Lord as great delight in burnt offerings and sacrifices,
> as in obedience to the voice of the Lord?
> Surely, to obey is better than sacrifice,
> and to heed than the fat of rams.[18]

This warning against this type of formalism which comes decades before the building of the temple in Jerusalem, even at this stage puts the emphasis on obedience and piety rather than strict sacrificial practices. Many prophets echoed the same message with great force and often in a radical voice. The following texts no need at all of commentary because their meaning is unmistakable.

Here is Micah extolling the importance of justice, mercy and of walking with God:

> With what shall I come before the Lord,
> and bow myself before God on high?
> Shall I come before him with burnt offerings,
> with calves a year old?
> Will the Lord be pleased with thousands of rams,
> with ten thousands of rivers of oil?
> Shall I give my firstborn for my transgression,
> the fruit of my body for the sin of my soul?
> He has told you, O mortal, what is good;
> and what does the Lord require of you
> but to do justice, and to love kindness,
> and to walk humbly with your God?[19]

Here is Amos, expressing God's disgust for sacrificial practices so great that he denies ever having anything to do with them in the desert:

> I hate, I despise your festivals,
> and I take no delight in your solemn assemblies.
> Even though you offer me your burnt offerings and grain offerings,

---

18. 1 Sam 15:22.
19. Mic 6:6–8.

The God Who Eats with His Own

> I will not accept them;
> and the offerings of well-being of your fatted animals
> I will not look upon.
> Take away from me the noise of your songs;
> I will not listen to the melody of your harps.
> But let justice roll down like waters,
> and righteousness like an ever-flowing stream.
>
> Did you bring to me sacrifices and offerings the forty years in the wilderness, O house of Israel? You shall take up Sakkuth your king, and Kaiwan your star-god, your images, which you made for yourselves; therefore I will take you into exile beyond Damascus, says the Lord, whose name is the God of hosts.[20]

Here is Hosea, saying that God wants rather that his people to know him, and—and amazingly this is the bottom line—that he cannot forgive the sins of the people because of their sacrifices!

> For I desire steadfast love and not sacrifice,
> the knowledge of God rather than burnt offerings.[21]
> When Ephraim multiplied altars to expiate sin,
> they became to him altars for sinning.
> Though I write for him the multitude of my instructions,
> they are regarded as a strange thing.
> Though they offer choice sacrifices,
> though they eat flesh,
> the Lord does not accept them.
> Now he will remember their iniquity,
> and punish their sins;
> they shall return to Egypt.[22]

Here is Jeremiah, where God despises the backsliding and excesses of his people:

---

20. Amos 5:21–27.
21. Hos 6:6.
22. Hos 8:11–13.

> Thus says the Lord of hosts, the God of Israel: Add your burnt offerings to your sacrifices, and eat the flesh. For in the day that I brought your ancestors out of the land of Egypt, I did not speak to them or command them concerning burnt offerings and sacrifices. But this command I gave them, "Obey my voice, and I will be your God, and you shall be my people; and walk only in the way that I command you, so that it may be well with you." Yet they did not obey or incline their ear, but, in the stubbornness of their evil will, they walked in their own counsels, and looked backward rather than forward.[23]

Other Voices Proclaiming Another Path

Isaiah, from the very first chapter of his great prophetic canvas, opens up another path. He recalls how fed up God was with the practice of sacrifices and the festival gatherings which had become pure form. In the manner of Micah and Amos, Isaiah pleads the case of widows and orphans. But he also introduces two new ideas: purification by water—not by blood—and engaging with the Lord: "Come and argue with me."

> What to me is the multitude of your sacrifices?
> says the Lord;
> I have had enough of burnt offerings of rams
> and the fat of fed beasts;
> I do not delight in the blood of bulls,
> or of lambs, or of goats.
> When you come to appear before me,
> who asked this from your hand?
> Trample my courts no more;
> bringing offerings is futile;
> incense is an abomination to me.
> New moon and sabbath and calling of convocation—
> I cannot endure solemn assemblies with iniquity.

---

23. Jer 7:21–24.

> Your new moons and your appointed festivals
> my soul hates;
> they have become a burden to me,
> I am weary of bearing them.
> When you stretch out your hands,
> I will hide my eyes from you;
> even though you make many prayers,
> I will not listen;
> your hands are full of blood.
> Wash yourselves; make yourselves clean;
> remove the evil of your doings
> from before my eyes;
> cease to do evil,
> learn to do good;
> seek justice,
> rescue the oppressed,
> defend the orphan,
> plead for the widow.
> Come now, let us argue it out,
> says the Lord[24]

This other path is the very same as that followed in Psalm 51. The penitent is ready to offer sacrifice to remove his sin but recognizes that God does not require it. He prays to him rather to cleanse and purify him. Water is the substitute for blood. The only sacrifice is a heart broken in the act of genuine confession.

> You desire truth in the inward being;
> therefore teach me wisdom in my secret heart.
> Purge me with hyssop, and I shall be clean;
> wash me, and I shall be whiter than snow.
> Let me hear joy and gladness;
> let the bones that you have crushed rejoice.
> Hide your face from my sins,

---

24. Isa 1:10–20.

> and blot out all my iniquities.
> Create in me a clean heart, O God,
> and put a new and right spirit within me.
> Do not cast me away from your presence,
> and do not take your holy spirit from me.
> Restore to me the joy of your salvation,
> and sustain in me a willing spirit . . .
> O Lord, open my lips,
> and my mouth will declare your praise.
> For you have no delight in sacrifice;
> if I were to give a burnt offering, you would not be pleased.
> The sacrifice acceptable to God is a broken spirit;
> a broken and contrite heart, O God, you will not despise.[25]

This might seem to be a radical change but in fact it is a return to their roots. For God's plan was never to allow sin to separate him from humans beings but rather to encounter them, whatever their circumstances and whatever their faults. Whenever sacrifice opens up a gap between God and the one who is offering it, when sacrifice wounds God as was so often the case, such long lapses, it is because there has been some awful malfunction. If only the Israelites had been able to hold on to the original revelation at the heart of the sacrificial system!

Sacrifice as a Shared Meal

God wishes to live among his people. That is what I have been trying hard to emphasize since the beginning of this book. God has the sanctuary built because he wishes to dwell among his own. But if there is no link between his wish to be present and the basic purpose of the sanctuary—sacrifice—then God's plan is shaky in the extreme. For the very opposite is true: the presence of God, the sanctuary, and sacrifice are inextricably linked. That is what God said to Moses at the end of his revelation on Sinai.

---

25. Ps 51:6–17.

The God Who Eats with His Own

The mountain is still smoking. The sound of the trumpet is still ringing in the ears of the Israelites. But the thunder is still and lightening no longer zigzags across the sky. Phew! When God speaks, they tremble! They thought they were done for. Fortunately God has now composed himself. But he still has things to say to Moses especially about the altar:

> The Lord said to Moses: "Thus you shall say to the Israelites: 'You have seen for yourselves that I spoke with you from heaven. You shall not make gods of silver alongside me, nor shall you make for yourselves gods of gold. You need make for me only an altar of earth and sacrifice on it your burnt offerings and your offerings of well being, your sheep and your oxen; in every place where I cause my name to be remembered I will come to you and bless you. But if you make for me an altar of stone, do not build it of hewn stones; for if you use a chisel upon it you profane it. You shall not go up by steps to my altar, so that your nakedness may not be exposed on it.'"[26]

These verses bring to an end the theophany of Sinai. Movements in space have meaning. On the one hand God speaks from on high to the earth. On the other, man must not approach the altar nor approach God. For God it is top-down. Never a grassroots operation by man. The Babylonians wanted to go up towards God. You can see why their religion became the symbol of great apostasy! Coming down is God's prerogative. It is his supreme will: he comes down to meet us. And when he comes it is purely to bless.

> When God comes, following a sacrifice, it is not to terrify the worshipper but to bless him. The coming of God to the pilgrim always ends in blessing . . . The whole point of sacrifice is that man should meet God. It is a privileged place of meeting between God and those faithful to him . . . It must be stated categorically: any interpretation which does not place blessing at the very heart of sacrifice must be considered non-biblical.[27]

---

26. Exod 20:22–26.
27. Grappe and Marx, *Le sacrifice*, 25 (translation mine).

At a time when there was no longer a sanctuary, such a dramatic approach by God helps us to understand what happens when God decides to pay a visit to human beings. It was exactly like this when God came to visit Abraham, sitting just outside his tent.[28]

It's hot, very hot. The air is heavy. Three men pop up out of nowhere. It is the Lord—three men—who appears, so says the beginning of the story. Theologians rub their hands at this: it is the Father, Son and Holy Spirit! Not so, for we discover later that of the three persons, two are messengers who will leave quickly for Sodom.[29] Do not seek further clarification. The text does not provide any. For this story tells of a group of guests, the Lord, two messengers and Abraham sharing a meal. It is completely unheard of. If you can understand what is happening here you have automatically won your ticket into heaven. God is eating with men! A man—and his whole tribe—who prepare a meal for God, who wait on him having first washes his feet. A man who displays his hospitality, his deference, his submission . . . "Do not pass by, I beg you, without gracing my home with your presence, me your servant!" The text does not use the language of sacrifice, but someone must have killed the calf in order to serve it up on the table. Abraham offered the tenderest cuts of veal—good food and food only, his very best.

In general terms this is what sacrifice is in the Old Testament.[30] It is the moment and the means chosen by God to come down to bless. It is the clearest indication by humans that they wish to welcome him and to have him honor them with his presence. From then on everything revolves around the altar, which after all is just a type of table. For a sacrifice is nothing but a meal offered to God. Not that he is hungry and must be fed. But it is the sign that we are ready to welcome him. It is a request that seeks benediction. "Come, do not pass by, stop, bless." The book of

---

28. Gen 18.

29. Gen 19:1.

30. On sacrifices in general, which is obviously a difficult topic, cf. Stroumsa, *End of Sacrifice*.

Deuteronomy expresses this idea very well. Once the high places had been destroyed God commands his people:

> But you shall seek the place that the Lord your God will choose out of all your tribes as his habitation to put his name there. You shall go there, bringing there your burnt offerings and your sacrifices, your tithes and your donations, your votive gifts, your freewill offerings, and the firstlings of your herds and flocks. And you shall eat there in the presence of the Lord your God, you and your households together, rejoicing in all the undertakings in which the Lord your God has blessed you.[31]

"Give me a call and we can go out to eat together." That's the sort of thing friends say today. God does not impose himself on us. He extends an invitation and awaits a reply. "God is inviting you to a banquet at Thoereion, tomorrow at nine o'clock"—thus reads a manuscript published some years ago.[32] Abraham had had to urge God to stay and eat with him. Reread the stories of apostasy and idolatry in the Old Testament. They also speak of banquets or perhaps one should say a kind of "anti-banquet." So, to take but one example from the book of Numbers, Israel follows after the God Baal of Peor: "While Israel was staying at Shittim, the people began to have sexual relations with the women of Moab. These invited the people to the sacrifices of their gods, and the people ate and bowed down to their gods."[33] In the same way we can understand why Daniel and his friends refused to eat the food offered by the king of Babylon. The four young resisted the temptation to idolatry. Rightly so.[34]

At the end of this memorable encounter "the Lord went his way and Abraham returned to his home." They fell into each other's arms. God squeezed tight, very tight. Then God embraced Abraham with the greatest tenderness. "Until we meet again, Abraham, until then." Had Abraham been blessed? It is a silly question. Just

31. Deut 12:5–7.
32. *Collectanea Papyrologica*, 315ff.
33. Num 25:1–2.
34. Dan 1.

imagine what he is going to tell his children snuggled up to him for the bedtime story!

- Ishmael, Isaac, and your sisters too, come here while I tell you a story.
- Father is it a true story?
- Yes it is a true story, amazing but true . . . One day I was sitting just by my tent . . .

What a story! Without a doubt this God will do anything to be close to his own dear ones.

Itinerary 6

David Wants God to Live in a Temple
From Nomads to Settlers

When they left Egypt the Israelites were gypsies who knew nothing other than a nomadic life. They lived in tents—a pretty insecure sort of life. They endured an unrelenting climate with suffocating heat all day long and Arctic temperatures at night. They survived on a subsistence diet. Their water was scarce and not always drinkable. It is not difficult to imagine the tensions and fights which were part of the overcrowding in such a community: between women over a jug of water accidently spilled; between men whose cattle were grazing on a neighbor's patch. Forty years of travelling on foot, is a long time especially towards the end. And on top of that they had a land to conquer: full of battle-hardened tribes who had to be thrown out by force of arms. Milk and honey had been promised by God. The milk has gone sour and the honey is not at all sweet!

Is this land really where this God wishes to be among his people? When everyone is together in the desert, in a space of a couple of thousand meters square, it is easy for God to "place" himself in the middle. But where exactly is the middle of the promised land? It is difficult to see how God can continue to guarantee his presence once the people are scattered throughout the land. It is true that the book of Exodus ends with the glory of the Lord filling the dwelling:

> Then the cloud covered the tent of meeting, and the glory of the Lord filled the tabernacle. Moses was not able to enter the tent of meeting because the cloud settled upon it, and the glory of the Lord filled the tabernacle. Whenever the cloud was taken up from the tabernacle, the Israelites would set out on each stage of their journey; but if the cloud was not taken up, then they did not set out until the day that it was taken up. For the cloud of the Lord was on the tabernacle by day, and fire was in the cloud by night, before the eyes of all the house of Israel at each stage of their journey.[1]

But after this account, the cloud disappears, dissolves.

Before occupying the land the people must undergo a sort of rite of passage: to leave the wilderness for good and occupy the promised land. The miraculous crossing of the River Jordan marks this transition. It will no longer be the cloud which leads the people and which confirms the presence of God but the sanctuary. Not the whole of the sanctuary but what you might consider the very heart of it, the sign of the very presence of God himself: the ark of the covenant. It is the ark which leads the way across the river. Sometime after it is the same ark which leads the way for the daily military march around the walls of Jericho. But when it comes to the victory at Ai, there is no reference to the ark. Instead we find that Joshua constructed an altar on Mount Ebal.[2]

The ark can also be found in the book of Samuel when we are told, "The word of the Lord was rare in those days; visions were not widespread."[3] No more cloud. Now silent God. What then remains of his wish to be present among them?

Now everything is focused on this box made from acacia, one hundred twenty-five centimeters long, seventy-five centimeters wide and seventy-five centimeters high. To get rid of the previous

1. Exod 40:34–38.
2. Jos 3:11.
3. 1 Sam 3:1.

David Wants God to Live in a Temple

inhabitants, the Philistines, it is best to guarantee the divine presence especially since the first battle with them had ended in a rout. So they decided: "Let us bring the ark of the covenant of the Lord here from Shiloh, so that he may come among us and save us from the power of our enemies."[4] In doing this, the Israelites just copied a common practice among the people around them: whenever you start a war, you better take your God with you as a protection. But, in this story, the lesson handed out by God is cruel: it is not a wooden box which can affirm his presence and guarantee victory. In spite of the ark Israel is beaten again. There are a thousand deaths and the ark is taken as spoils of war. The news of its capture is terrible. Eli the priest sees it as a fatal blow; his daughter-in-law, wife of his sin Phineas, killed in combat, suddenly goes into labor. Totally helpless, she gives the son who has just been born a name which evokes this disaster: Ichabod; the ark has been seized.[5] The glory of the Lord—the Lord himself—has departed the land. So much for the presence of God among his people!

The Philistines are about to discover the sad reality that this wooden chest is a bit of a handicap. The god Dagon will not be at all happy at the prospect of having it placed next to him. It even causes him to fall on the ground several times. The Philistine council of ministers has to meet several times. They want to get rid of this wretched furniture. From Ashdod, the ark goes to Gath then to Eqron. At every stage there is panic. After seven months of this Philistine pilgrimage, the ark arrives at Beth-Shemesh, the field of Joshua. The result is no better: seventy deaths among the Israelite men. It is at Kiriath-Yearim, home to Abinadab, that the ark finally comes to rest. Eliezer was appointed to keep guard over it.[6]

---

4. 1 Sam 4:3.
5. See 1 Sam 4:1–22.
6. See 1 Sam 6 and 7 for the whole story.

The Ark Arrives in Jerusalem

The saga of this ark which nobody has any idea how to handle, illustrates clearly the political instability which characterized Israel when they entered the promised land. Precisely because settling has not been easy. And its religious life has unavoidably been affected by the upheaval. The scattering of tribes throughout the land has been accompanied by a fragmentation in their religion. They are seeking God. But there is no cloud. No sanctuary. Where on earth has he gone? They search for him desperately. A man called Micah (not the prophet) "had a shrine, and he made an ephod and teraphim, and installed one of his sons, a his priest."[7] He even took on a young Levite in the belief that God would now be with him.

It is no surprise then, that the author of the book of Judges introduces this period with the following phrase: "In those days there was no king in Israel; all the people did what was right in their own eyes."[8] When kings were appointed, they were supposed to put an end to all this. After the death of Saul events unravel quickly: the enthronement of King David by all the tribes of Israel gathered at Hebron; the capture of the city of Jerusalem which becomes the new capital; a stunning victory over the Philistines.[9]

But much more importantly, David's task was to bring the ark of the covenant back to Jerusalem The many precautions he took show how fearful he was. The terrible fate of Uzzah, struck down on the spot for trying to prevent the ark from falling sometime earlier, still preyed on people's minds. To forestall the divine thunder, David makes sure that the procession stops every six steps to offer a bull and another animal as sacrifices. Once the precious ark is put down in the tent erected for the purpose, David offers sacrifices and peace offerings—probably offerings of pure relief—before blessing the people. But this young king was rather presumptuous! Usually it is God who gives the order to put up a sacred tent. Usually it is

7. Judg 17:5.
8. Judg 17:6.
9. 1 Sam 5.

he who offers benediction after the sacrifice. But when David got home, there was a serious argument with his wife Mikal because he had uncovered himself before the eyes of his maidservants. It all ended in a divorce. She will no longer enjoy the favor of the king as long as she lives.[10] It is better to begin a reign like this.

The Social, Political and Religious Situation

His majesty David settles in his royal palace in Jerusalem, which he calls a "house of cedar." But the ark of God is actually on the campground at Mount Zion, in the tent. David thinks it through intelligently. There is something here which does not make sense and it needs to be resolved—fast. God deserves something better: a temple to house the holy ark. Nathan approves the royal project. The temple gets the go-ahead! But during the night God appears. He has something to say about the king's plan.[11] But before we hear what that is, we must set the text in its general context, political, and religious.

David has conquered Jerusalem in order to make it his capital. What modern historians and archaeologists call the city of David is a minute parcel of land nestling on the sides of Mount Zion: at most five hundred meters long by two hundred meters wide. This is different from the proportions and magnificence of certain cities in the Near East, like Babylon or Nineveh, let alone Athens in Europe. Every one of these cities had one temple at the very least, often several. All of these cities thought of themselves as the center of the universe. So for example, Babylon says it is the center of the world, the very point of contact between heaven and earth, symbolized in the great ziggurat. Mircea Eliade puts it this way:

> The architectonic symbolism of the Center may be formulated as follows:
> 1. The Sacred Mountain—where heaven and earth meet—is situated at the center of the world.

---

10. 2 Sam 6:20–23.
11. See 2 Sam 7, to which I will refer constantly in the following pages.

2. Every temple or palace—and, by extension, every sacred city or royal residence—is a Sacred Mountain, thus becoming a Center.[12]

The Talmud describes the creation of the universe this way: "We were taught in accord with the view that the world was started [created] from Zion on."[13]

So it is not by chance that David set his capital, Zion, on the top of a hill. The center of his world cannot be a modest affair. The higher the better. Otherwise like Babylon with its lowland setting, it would be necessary to build a very high tower to show that it does indeed reach to heaven.

A capital without a temple is no capital. A capital without a temple cannot be the center of the world. A capital without a temple is a like a wild desert place, inhabited by demonic forces. So David needs a temple so that he can authenticate a holy space where earth meets heaven. Jerusalem will no longer be a small township plundered by the Jebusites, the previous occupants, but the center of the universe.

But David also has political reasons for building a temple. His nomadic people have a tendency to live in isolation from each other. It is important to find some political cement that will unite these tribes who are so quick to make war on each other. His royal authority is also at stake. Without a capital or a temple he would just be a cardboard king. Many kings past and present had long understood that in order to stamp their authority and power on the people it was vital to build a temple in their capital. Thus the Babylonian king Nabopolassar in the seventh century BCE prayed to the god Marduk:

> I rebuilt for the mistress of Sippar, the exalted princess, my princess . . . a temple wherein she might find peace of mind, and I made it brilliant as the day. In the future, O mistress of Sippar, powerful mistress, when I have brought this temple to a state of completion, and thou hast taken up thy dwelling therein, do thou establish

12. Eliade, *Myth of the Eternal Return*, 12.
13. *Yomah* 54b.

me, Nabopolassar, the king, thy restorer, forever like the bricks of Sippar and Babylon; and do thou permit my sovereignty to last into far future days.[14]

And well before him Goudea, king of Lagash, erected a temple for the god Ningirsu in the third millennium. The steps in his project are clearly set out in five cylinders discovered by archaeologists. It all corresponds very closely with the course followed by David and Solomon: the precondition of divine authorization followed by the building project, the dedication ceremony, the divine blessing.[15] All historians agree on this point: in the ancient Near East, royalty and the construction of temples are inextricably bound up with each other. So for David this building project is vital.

House of David—House of God

Chapter 7 of the second book of Samuel, which describes the intentions of David, is an extraordinary and formidable text. It is also one of the most difficult to understand. Theologians have long pulled their hair out over this chapter. It is unwise and probably counterproductive to engage in all their debates.

I have every reason to think that this text reaches into heaven. But when you reach for the heavens you had better be inspired as the author of these lines certainly was. To read it at a surface level, with the critical faculties silenced, is not enough here. Using the tools of narratology, we will find that several salient points emerge.

Narratology is the literary discipline which studies the techniques and structures used by the author when constructing a story. For thirty years or so this discipline has been applied to the study of biblical texts, beginning in the United States, then in Europe particularly in the French-speaking part of the continent, notably under the influence of Daniel Marguerat and Yvan Bourquin.[16] According to narratologists all stories develop in five stages:

14. Bruce, *Inscription of Nabopolassar*, no. III, col. ii, 5–20, 186.
15. Hallo, *Context of Scripture*, vol. II, 429–33.
16. Marguerat and Bourquin, *How to Read Bible Stories*, esp. chap. 4.

1. The initial situation which provides the reader with the basic information: Who? What? Why? What is the problem?
2. The complication (nouement) which contains an attempt to relieve the tension or solve the problem.
3. The transforming action which brings a solution to the problem.
4. The "dénouement" (unraveling) of the story which is the exact opposite of the original solution.
5. The final situation where the initial problem is resolved.

Second Samuel 7, viewed through the prism of this method, highlights the main hinges on which the principal teachings of this text turn.

1. Initial situation: David lives in a house of cedar, but the ark of God is merely under canvas.
2. Complication: David decides that he must build a house for the Lord.
3. Transforming action: God says that he has never commanded any such thing despite the nod given by the prophet Nathan.
4. Dénouement: God replies to David: "It is I who am going to build a house for David."
5. Final situation: David thanks God for taking the initiative. He has understood that it is indeed God who will build a house for him.

We can now go into the detail of the story. There is a great deal riding on our understanding of this text.

The beginning of the chapter highlights very clearly the installation of David in his capital. Peace reigns in Israel, at last. There is no need for any royal fireman to put out fire after fire to contain any hubs of insurrection or revolt. There are no enemies around any longer. The king is comfortably settled in his cedar house at the heart of his little center-of-the-world capital. He is no longer a shepherd who crisscrosses the country behind his flocks.

David Wants God to Live in a Temple

He is now properly settled. What David wants now is that God will settle, too. For good. For if God does not call Jerusalem his home then his royal authority and the prestige of his capital are very vulnerable. David says, "It has turned out well for me, Lord, and I want it to turn out well for you too. Allow me to build you a cedar house. I am determined to build a house, a temple."

But God refused to be confined by settlement. The rhetorical question ("Are you the one to build me a house to live in?"[17]) only serves to underline the categorical nature of God's refusal. Twice God reminds his people that he also is a "displaced person" like all the Israelites.[18] He is a nomad like them. He never expected to be anything else. He promised to give a land to his people but he never sought a place, even a sacred space, for himself. It is true that he says that he is going to identify a place but not for himself: for his people Israel.[19]

God does not content himself with this categorical refusal. He goes to the heart of the matter. He is not against the idea of building a house. But he will not have a project like this imposed upon him. Must he remind them that it was he who took the initiative to build a sanctuary in the first place? Again he says to David that if there is to be a house built it is he who will take charge of the project. To David's vow "I will build you a house," the Lord responds with, "The Lord will make you a house. When your days are fulfilled and you lie down with your ancestors, I will raise up your offspring after you, who shall come forth from your body, and I will establish his kingdom."[20] One house against another. But not at all in the same league!

David's plans included terracing, huge stone works, many teams of artisans, a building site employing hundreds and hundreds of workers. Noise, sweat, dust. He would have to put the finance in place and keep within budget. This is a sort of high finance investment. God's plan is quite different. No stone, no cement, no wood,

17. 2 Sam 7:5.
18. 2 Sam 7:6–7.
19. 2 Sam 7:10.
20. 2 Sam 7:11–12.

no precious metals. It is about a person, a descendant who will sit on the throne of David. And not just one but a line of descendants because the promise is eternal: "Your house and your kingdom shall be made sure forever before me; your throne shall be established forever."[21] This puts an end to every royal nightmare, the fear of a common bastard child or a lowborn usurper taking over. From now on, all fear is banished, the succession guaranteed for ever.

The reply is so different from the one which David was expecting that you wonder whether he understood. The posture of the king as he comes before the Lord seems to indicate that he has got the message. He asks not a single question nor does he make the slightest comment on his own suggested project: building a temple. But he does not cease thanking God for his goodness, for his kindness to his family and his people, and for working to liberate them.

Except that . . . except that verse 13 halts the narrative flow in such a way as to cast doubt on the interpretation we have just made. It says, "It is he [Solomon] who will build a house in my name, and I will establish his royal throne forever." This verse goes against the stream of the whole of the rest of the chapter, that for most interpreters, it can only be an interpolation, something later inserted into the story to justify the eventual construction of the temple by Solomon. A single verse favoring the building of the temple embedded in a chapter twenty-nine verses long which speaks basically of the Davidic dynasty as the one true house built by the Lord. The text is difficult. As a reader, you could well get lost at this point.

The idea of an interpolation may seem incongruous. Could a guilty malicious hand have introduced this verse in the original story? Should one start worrying that if one applies this method to other texts, it could seriously alter the content of the biblical revelation? To demonize this possible explanation is not going to advance the debate. Interpolation or not, this is not the only time when biblical texts express an idea which is not in line with the

---

21. 2 Sam 7:16–17.

divine will. The book of Job provides another example: it consists in large part of the speeches of Job's friends who, we later learn, have misrepresented God.[22]

So, I repeat, there is a great deal riding on this text. God says quite clearly that he favors a royal dynasty over a building, a dynasty resulting ultimately in a messiah. He says quite clearly that no one is going to confine him within walls made by men. David got the point all right. He understood that God's plan far surpassed his own petty ideas. But when Nathan left the royal palace and left him alone, I imagine David reassessing the project, as any human king saying to God: "Yes but on the other hand, Lord, you cannot stay in a tent. How will I look in a capital without a temple?" If there is indeed an interpolation it underlines how difficult it is for humans to accept the plan of God. Finally this "interpolated" verse is very much in line with the theology of the books of Chronicles that later rewrite the whole history of David eliminating his mistakes, because their theological project is different. This verse thirteen confirms an historical fact: Solomon did indeed build the house of the Lord. Solomon was the first to fulfill the promise that there would always be a son of David on the royal throne.

So Solomon built the temple. And if I may, with a hint of a twinkle in my eye, just make a small point of geopolitics: when it was finished, the outside of the small Jebusite settlement was more than doubled. The esplanade of the temple was now bigger than the city of David.

So for better or worse, actually for better *and* worse, Solomon built the temple.[23]

---

22. Job 42:7.
23. For a sound analysis of 2 Sam 7, cf. Jan Rück, "Une dynastie en crise," 81–97.

ITINERARY 7

Solomon Builds the Temple...
and Destroys the Monarchy

THE REIGN OF SOLOMON lasted forty years like that of his father David. Forty years retold in eleven chapters.[1] The editor has inevitably had to make some choices. The story is carefully constructed. It is a great saga, a story to be listened to, read aloud in public. We must remember that in the time of the Old Testament, and until at least the third century CE only a very small minority of the population—less than 10 percent—were able to read a text. We must also remember that use of the sacred scrolls containing the text was limited to public ceremonial occasions, in the temple and then later in the synagogues. Private ownership of a scroll was a rare exception and only possible for the very wealthy.

Nowadays we read in silence in our heads. Written documents are made up of conventional symbols set down on paper. Reading involves looking at and decoding the text. At this time however one approached the text not through the eyes but the ears. Texts are a collection of sounds. As a result it was important for the author to use a certain number of devices to make himself understood: repetition of the most important words and themes; use of refrains; easily remembered structures. Even if you

---

1. 1 Kgs 1–11.

can retrace your steps in personal reading you cannot do that with the spoken word. Orality requires great concentration. The author must help the listener to lose nothing. Once the text has been read, nothing is left beyond the imprint resonating in the mind of those who have heard it. What do you hear then as you listen to the saga of King Solomon?

The Builder-King

The very least you can say is that Solomon is presented as a builder-king. No less than four chapters are devoted to the construction of the temple.[2] What is striking is that the story makes everything revolve around him. It is true that Hiram, king of Tyre, comes to give him a helping hand.[3] But although thirty thousand Israelites were pressed into service, not counting seventy thousand porters and eighty thousand stonecutters, none of them is mentioned by name. Solomon does everything. Solomon Contractor: masonry, structural work, roofing, flooring, sculpting in gold, carpentry. Moses had done it differently. Or rather God had done it differently for the construction of the sanctuary in the wilderness:

> Then Moses said to the Israelites: See, the Lord has called by name Bezalel son of Uri son of Hur, of the tribe of Judah; he has filled him with divine spirit, with skill, intelligence, and knowledge in every kind of craft, to devise artistic designs, to work in gold, silver, and bronze, in cutting stones for setting, and in carving wood, in every kind of craft. And he has inspired him to teach, both him and Oholiab son of Ahisamach, of the tribe of Dan. He has filled them with skill to do every kind of work done by an artisan or by a designer or by an embroiderer in blue, purple, and crimson yarns, and in fine linen, or by a weaver—by any sort of artisan or skilled designer.[4]

---

2. 1 Kgs 5–8.
3. 1 Kgs 5:15–26.
4. Exod 35:30–35.

Does this mean that Solomon's project is purely of human origin? Certainly not.

The Wise King

The same God who has filled Bezalel and Oholiab with the spirit of wisdom, intelligence and knowledge for all sorts of works is the same God who gives Solomon "a wise and discerning heart."[5] The beginning of his reign appears as a rise in power, a growth in wisdom. The height is attained when the Queen of Sheba comes to Jerusalem on a state visit to this king whose reputation knows no limits. "The report was true that I heard in my own land of your accomplishments and of your wisdom, but I did not believe the reports until I came and my own eyes had seen it. Not even half had been told me; your wisdom and prosperity far surpass the report that I had heard."[6]

I must however admit that, purely based on the books of Kings, this wisdom of Solomon is not that impressive. I would prefer to turn to several concrete examples of his words of wisdom without having to resort to the book of Proverbs, a few psalms and the Song of Songs. It is true that the story of the two mothers who are fighting over their baby and the way in which Solomon sought a just settlement shows that this king is not only very intelligent but also has a heart.[7] But I have the clear impression that his wisdom and intelligence are mainly described in terms of his ability to bring to completion the great work of building the temple. Nonetheless, seven years of work in total . . . for one hundred eighty thousand workers. When it comes to competitiveness, he is far from the best!

---

5. 1 Kgs 3:12.
6. 1 Kgs 10:6–7.
7. 1 Kgs 3:16–28.

Not Only a Temple but Also a Palace

Anyone who works on building sites will tell you: tricks, fiddles, the syphoning off of materials, theft are sadly standard practice, particularly when a single large company manages the project. Rumors circulate in many cities about luxurious houses and villas that strangely spring up at the same time as for example a new metro line or large public building. Nothing is more amazing than the heavy plant driver, or a team of painters or tilers: they can disappear, and then reappear on another building site, entirely as their whim.

What malicious hand has placed the first verses of 1 Kings 7 of the Solomon saga just before the climax in chapter 8 and the inauguration of the temple? What are we meant to think here? Seven years of public works for the temple, but thirteen years of works for the house of Solomon.[8] Solomon is wise, it is true, but not to the point of forgetting his own vested interests. Furthermore have you ever compared the measurements of the royal palace with those of the temple? Let me convert the biblical measurements into meters: thirty meters long, ten meters wide, fifteen meters high for the temple.[9] Fifty meters long, twenty-five-meters wide, fifteen meters high for the king's palace.[10] Almost twice as long, twice as wide. The same height for the gentleman's palace as for the temple of the Lord. And that is not all. Solomon also builds a house for his wife, daughter of a pharaoh.[11] Solomon Company for building of all types—palaces and temples!

The Strange Temple Inauguration Ceremony

"Then Solomon assembled the elders of Israel and all the heads of the tribes, the leaders of the ancestral houses of the Israelites,

---

8. 1 Kgs 7:1.
9. 1 Kgs 6:2.
10. 1 Kgs 7:2.
11. 1 Kgs 7:8.

before King Solomon in Jerusalem, to bring up the ark of the covenant of the Lord out of the city of David, which is Zion."[12]

A required part of the inauguration of the temple is that the ark of the covenant must be set down inside the newly constructed building. That was exactly what David had in mind: build permanent structure to house the ark of the covenant. There are some important dignitaries representing the people—politicians and other VIPs—at the ceremony which reminds us that it has a political dimension: the tribes and clans of Israel must be bound together with unbreakable ties. This is an ideal opportunity in festivities that will stretch over no less than two weeks.[13] Hardly had the ark been set down in its place, "a cloud filled the house of the Lord, so that the priests could not stand to minister because of the cloud; for the glory of the Lord filled the house of the Lord."[14] What an extraordinary scene. You can imagine just how it impressed, even terrified those who were there on Mount Zion. This legendary cloud which had found a voice, not once but many times. They had heard the story of the holy cloud which had led the people for forty years. They had heard of the cloud which filled the wilderness dwelling. They also recalled that sadly it had disappeared as soon as they reached the promised land. And here it forms again on Mount Zion in this sumptuous temple which Solomon has just completed. You can hear the alleluias and the amens. "Glory to the Lord. He has come back among us. At last." And not a moment too soon after four hundred thirty years of being away! And Solomon immediately drives home the point. God will not allow them to fall a second time: "I have built you an exalted house, a place for you to dwell in forever."[15] Stay here, Lord. Don't move an inch. Here then is the God who is always moving on now under house arrest, forever.

After this moment of intense emotion Solomon begins his inaugural address. And it is a very strange address where the

12. 1 Kgs 8:1.
13. 1 Kgs 8:65.
14. 1 Kgs 8:10–11.
15. 1 Kgs 8:13.

words of God and those of the king are mixed. When you analyze them carefully the words of God are not the most appropriate in the circumstances: "Since the day that I brought my people Israel out of Egypt, I have not chosen a city from any of the tribes of Israel in which to build a house, that my name might be there; but I chose David to be over my people Israel."[16] God states clearly his preference, his choice: no capital. No temple in the city. But rather someone, a king to guide the people. I can well imagine some raised eyebrows at these words among the public gathered on the esplanade. A king but no temple? So what are we doing here? Fortunately—or unfortunately—Solomon continues: "My father David had it in mind to build a house for the name of the Lord, the God of Israel."[17] Wow, there we have it: the temple. End of the (very) short inaugural address—one should always be brief in such circumstances following Solomon's fine example. Time now for the prayer.

What is striking about Solomon's prayer is his reference to the divine promise. It is worth repeating that what is at stake here is asking God to bless this temple and honor it with his presence (which he has already done through the appearance of the cloud). But Solomon just like his father David at the beginning understood very well what the promise represents. He repeats it without any hesitation: "O Lord, God of Israel, keep for your servant my father David that which you promised him, saying, 'There shall never fail you a successor before me to sit on the throne of Israel, if only your children look to their way, to walk before me as you have walked before me.' Therefore, O God of Israel, let your word be confirmed, which you promised to your servant my father David."[18]

It is clearly the royal succession which is at stake, before anything else. But, like David his father, Solomon will quickly slip from the kingship to the building of the temple. With the same embarrassment too.

16. 1 Kgs 8:16.
17. 1 Kgs 8:17.
18. 1 Kgs 8:25–26.

God had answered to David's idea to build a temple by a rhetorical question: 'Are you the one to build me a house to live in?'[19] Solomon did not forget. He sings on the shame hymn sheet, with a rhetorical question to God: "Will God indeed dwell on the earth? Even heaven and the highest heaven cannot contain you, much less this house that I have built!"[20]

Has there ever been a more offbeat prayer? Here is a king who has gathered all the dignitaries and power brokers in his country. Here is a king who stands in front of his people ready for the official inauguration of the temple. Here is a king who has just witnessed God's response to his grand project expressed in the miraculous appearance of the cloud. But a king who can find nothing else to say than that God will not dwell in this place! And he is supposed to be wise and intelligent too! My thoughts go out to the one hundred eighty thousand workers who have sweated for seven years over the construction of this sumptuous building. I hear some of them whispering, barely audible: "All that for this?"

This question is not prompted by some clumsy expression uttered by Solomon in the heat of the moment. What follows only serves to confirm the king's words. One sentence echoes as a refrain no less than eight times before the prayer ends: "O hear in heaven your dwelling place."[21] Yes Solomon has clearly understood: God has no intention of living in a house built by a man however wise he may be. And when prayers are addressed to him in this place he will reply from his own dwelling—invisible and immaterial—located in the heavens. Solomon has spoken true even if he has sawn off a branch he has tried very hard to grow for the better part of his reign. God will bring upon him a deep sleep. In a second dream he appears to him once more.

---

19. 2 Sam 7:5.
20. 1 Kgs 8:27–28.
21. 1 Kgs 8:30, 32, 34, 36, 39, 43, 45, 49.

God's Response to Solomon's Prayer

God's response to Solomon's prayer has a strange ring: "I have heard your prayer and your plea, which you made before me; I have consecrated this house that you have built, and put my name there forever."[22] Listen carefully to God's reply. He does not promise to dwell in this place. He only promises to lend his name to it. Let me offer a comparison. From my office in Binfield (Berkshire, UK) I can see a huge and highly desirable residence hidden among the trees, surrounded by a track for training racehorses. The estate belongs to one of the richest men in the world, the Sultan of Brunei. The house bears his name. But he never lives there. So it is with the temple in Jerusalem. It bears the name of a God who lives elsewhere. But make no mistake: even though he does not live there, this house is not a watering hole for anyone who is drifting by. Warning: private property, protected by security.

Holy ground? It should be that. We expect that. In his last revelation to Solomon, God will set strict rules of access to the temple. This is the Lord's sanctuary. Please respect this place and observe silence. But there's nothing of all that. God will announce his conditions but they will have nothing to do with the place itself. God is adamant especially when it comes to matters of salvation: he has no intention of ignoring the substance of his promise to David. His obsession is the royal succession. He is thinking way beyond this building in Jerusalem. He is God, he can see into the distance. Well beyond this building, the heir apparent, the Messiah, the fulfillment of the promise is stirring.[23] God lays down some "ifs" to remind Solomon of the vital points: walk before him; obey his orders to the letter; keep his ordinances and his laws.[24] A number of "ifs" and terrible threats to anyone who strays away from him:

> If you turn aside from following me, you or your children, and do not keep my commandments and my statutes that

22. 1 Kgs 9:3.
23. 1 Kgs 9:5.
24. 1 Kgs 9:4–5.

I have set before you, but go and serve other gods and worship them, then I will cut Israel off from the land that I have given them; and the house that I have consecrated for my name I will cast out of my sight; and Israel will become a proverb and a taunt among all peoples. This house will become a heap of ruins; everyone passing by it will be astonished, and will hiss; and they will say, "Why has the Lord done such a thing to this land and to this house?" Then they will say, "Because they have forsaken the Lord their God, who brought their ancestors out of the land of Egypt, and embraced other gods, worshiping them and serving them; therefore the Lord has brought this disaster upon them."[25]

This temple which God really did not want, but which was built at Solomon's whim, becomes like a gauge to measure the faithfulness of the people. If they remain faithful, this house will be indestructible and shine brightly from the top of Mount Zion. If on the other hand it became dulled by infidelity, it would become a heap of stones and be the laughing stock of all surrounding nations.

It is a sinister message. God already knows what is going to happen. It did not take very long for the disaster to unfold.

Solomon, the King of Divided Love

"Solomon loved the Lord."[26] Four moving words which are not used very often to describe relationships between human beings and God. But words which are heard by those listening to the story of Solomon. After the troubled period of the judges, after the many battles in which King David was involved, these listeners begin to hope that at last now with Solomon they are on the right track. But once the temple was inaugurated and the promise repeated, things only go from bad to worse. What had been put into place little by little at the beginning of his reign is now dismantled. Solomon had

25. 1 Kgs 9:6–9.
26. 1 Kgs 3:3.

to get rid of his enemies: his brother Adonias, the priest Abiathar, Joab, the head of state, Shimei, an ally of Saul.[27]

But what is one to understand from the narrator in the books of Kings? "King Solomon loved many foreign women."[28] Solomon is going to put on again the hat of building site manager. It is for love of the Lord that he built him a temple. But it is also for love—for forbidden love—that he is going to build on the mountain facing Mount Zion a high place for Kemosh and one for Molech.[29] It is a descent into hell. The Lord turns against Solomon. Like a cheated wife he rejects this king of divided love. It will be Hadad the Edomite who will who will get in Solomon's way, aided by Rezon. Then it is Jeroboam, a member of the royal court, who secedes, with the blessing of the prophet Ahiya. And yet had not God appeared twice to Solomon? Twice![30]

It is a tragic end to a king who had begun so promisingly.

A Temple Standing but a Dynasty in Ruins

What is left at the end of Solomon's reign? A temple standing. A magnificent dwelling place on the summit of Mount Zion, its marble dazzling under the Judean sun. Solomon had wanted this temple, just like his father David. From his nearby palace he could, at the end of his life, behold it with the greatest satisfaction. It was he who had made it happen.

But God has another plan whereby it is a royal dynasty which is of importance—not a building. It is a disastrous end to the book of Kings: the temple stands proud and lofty. But the royal dynasty is in the dust. Schism, disunity, ferocious struggles between north and south are about to be unleashed.

What a paradox! God is no longer in a tent on the Mount Zion campsite. He has a beautiful temple just beside the royal

27. 1 Kgs 2.
28. 1 Kgs 11:1.
29. 1 Kgs 11:7–8.
30. 1 Kgs 11:9.

palace. But the one who has always chosen to live among his people is about to leave. Dark clouds gather on the horizon. There will follow a succession of kings, not only in Jerusalem but also in Samaria, capital of the northern kingdom. They for the most part will be a long way from the divine ideal. Some forty kings of whom only a handful—eight in all—will deserve the accolade he "did what was right in the sight of the Lord."[31] Thus God will not often be in good company in Jerusalem. Living in such mixed company is not going to be easy for him.

---

31. Among them Jehoash, king of Judah. Cf. 1 Kgs 12:1–3.

ITINERARY 8

Jeremiah and Illusory Confidence in the Temple

THE PROPHETIC MINISTRY OF Jeremiah begins probably in 627 BCE. He comes from a priestly family in Anathoth. His ancestors, the great priests Eli and Abiathar fared badly in the time of David and Solomon.[1] But at least he knows of the temple!

Jeremiah lives in a very troubled political period. He cannot escape the memory of the lot of the ten northern tribes, when the town of Samaria was taken and destroyed by the Assyrians, and a section of its population was deported to Babylon. At the moment the kingdom of Judah and of course the city of Jerusalem and its temple are being shunted back and forth between the great neighboring powers. The Assyrians as ever, but also the Babylonians and the Egyptians. Now it is a well-known fact that when times are bad the churches fill up. It is nothing new. So when Judah feels itself under threat, it is towards Jerusalem and the temple that everyone turns. God lives there, in that dwelling on top of Mount Zion, so the people are safe. There is nothing to fear. After all is that not exactly why the temple was built? That is a terrible mistake, so says Jeremiah. Now that is no way to attract the plaudits of the people whose national pride he has now wounded.

1. 1 Sam 2:27–36; 1 Kgs 2:26.

The Temple Covering of Sin

Chapter 7 of the book of Jeremiah delivers a message of great importance confirming the great misgivings already noted about the temple from the time of its construction to its inauguration. Here is the text in full with my own subtitles added:

Marching Orders

The word that came to Jeremiah from the Lord: Stand in the gate of the Lord's house, and proclaim there this word, and say, Hear the word of the Lord, all you people of Judah, you that enter these gates to worship the Lord. Thus says the Lord of hosts, the God of Israel:[2]

God's Exhortation

Amend your ways and your doings, and let me dwell with you in this place. Do not trust in these deceptive words: "This is the temple of the Lord, the temple of the Lord, the temple of the Lord."[3]

I Could Live Here If . . .

. . . you truly amend your ways and your doings, if you truly act justly one with another, if you do not oppress the alien, the orphan, and the widow, or shed innocent blood in this place, and if you do not go after other gods to your own hurt, then I will dwell with you in this place, in the land that I gave of old to your ancestors forever and ever. Here you are, trusting in deceptive words to no avail. Will you steal, murder, commit adultery, swear falsely, make offerings to Baal, and go after other gods that you have not known, and then come and stand before me in this house, which is called by my name, and say, "We are safe!"—only to go on doing all these

---

2. Jer 7:1–3.
3. Jer 7:3–4.

abominations? Has this house, which is called by my name, become a den of robbers in your sight? You know, I too am watching, says the Lord.[4]

See What Awaits You If You Do Not Change

Go now to my place that was in Shiloh, where I made my name dwell at first, and see what I did to it for the wickedness of my people Israel. And now, because you have done all these things, says the Lord, and when I spoke to you persistently, you did not listen, and when I called you, you did not answer, therefore I will do to the house that is called by my name, in which you trust, and to the place that I gave to you and to your ancestors, just what I did to Shiloh. And I will cast you out of my sight, just as I cast out all your kinsfolk, all the offspring of Ephraim.[5]

End of Jeremiah's Mission

> As for you, do not pray for this people, do not raise a cry or prayer on their behalf, and do not intercede with me, for I will not hear you.[6]

This passage is put together like echoing voices. Some words and expressions are used twice.

The first echo: "trust in deceptive words." What are these words? The text leaves us in no doubt: an ungodly confidence in the temple. Let me add: an ungodly confidence in the temple as the house of God. Or, as in the time of the judges, an unholy confidence in the temple as a protective shield guaranteeing victory against all comers. The second reference to confidence in false promises is even more radical. This kind of trust is useless, quite useless—be very clear about that, says the Lord.

4. Jer 7:5–11.
5. Jer 7:12–15.
6. Jer 7:16.

The second echo, "amend," reverberates as a call for change. It includes terms and conditions. But we know very well that the people have not budged an inch and reform . . . there has been none.

The third echo returns as a list of moral and spiritual dysfunctions:

- An absence of justice at the very heart of the people;
- Oppression of the immigrant, the orphan, the widow;
- Violence even in the temple, where innocent blood is spilt;
- Worship of other gods.

This list reverberates in the sound of verbs, doing words, or rather misdoing words:

- Stealing;
- Murdering;
- Committing adultery;
- Making false promises;
- Offering incense;
- Following other gods.

As for the fourth echoing voice, the whole dilemma shouts loud and clear: Is God going to live in this temple? Is God going to come to be in the midst of his people as he has always promised? Curiously the Lord does not promise to remain within the holy precincts. He only promises to let the people enjoy the land which he has given them. The Lord engages in a play on words here, for the word "place" in Hebrew is highly charged theologically speaking. He can identify somewhere which is no ordinary place, not even a temple.[7] This is what God says: "You believe that I dwell in this place but I do not. I will leave you in this place, this land that I have given you. But there is one condition and that is the deep

---

7. Judaism uses the same word (*maqom*) to designate God himself. See the Babylonian Talmud: *Ber.* 5:1, and *Sotah* 8:1, among many other examples.

reform which I have just outlined to you. Unless there is radical change, I will not leave you in this place which has been acquired at such cost."

As soon as Jeremiah delivers his message, the reason is clear. This is no conditional prophecy that leaves the door open to repentance. "I have called unceasingly but you have not answered" says the Lord. God left a message, any number of messages on Israel's answerphone but they never picked them up. Never called back. "He's calling us again. Why doesn't he just hang up."

So God asks Jeremiah to move the people to Shiloh. Shiloh, a charming little town in Samaria. The resting place of the ark of covenant for several years. It is where the young Samuel heard the call of God. A lovely settlement where they had constructed a sanctuary. But of Shiloh nothing remains, not one stone left on another.

Jerusalem delenda est, as Cato will later say of ancient Carthage: Jerusalem will be destroyed just as Shiloh has been destroyed. Or more accurately: the temple will be destroyed. And its destruction will symbolize the apostasy of Israel. Pierre-Maurice Bogaert captures the situation perfectly:

> People nurture the illusion that God's presence in his temple would give immunity against the punishment for crimes and offenses. Therefore, God needs to bring the people back to reality by destroying his temple. If the temple is used as a cover for immorality, then God's only option is to destroy it. This is the deep logic of the oracle.[8]

God will punish the people who wrongly put his confidence in the temple. He will not stay with them and will destroy the temple. Not only will God no longer dwell in the temple in Jerusalem but Israel will no longer inhabit the land. It is the end of the Holy City. End of the temple. End of the chosen people in their own land. Exile is at the door. Seventy awful years which will leave their indelible mark on Israel. And during all this time where will God be?

---

8. Bogaert, "La demeure de Dieu," 223 (translation mine).

ITINERARY 9

Ezekiel, the Priest Without a Temple

EZEKIEL, LIKE JEREMIAH, IS another prophet who should have been a priest. But he never was—and for good reason. Ezekiel was one of the ten thousand strong elite who had been deported to Babylon at the time of the capture of Jerusalem.[1] He would spend all his life in exile without ever seeing his home city again, or without ever officiating again in the temple. Ezekiel had felt it in his bones that his colleague Jeremiah's message was right: any confidence in the temple in Jerusalem was misguided. The unfaithfulness of his people had led God to destroy this place to indicate to them his rejection of them. Ezekiel is a priest without a temple. And yet you could say that even he recognized the credentials of the temple, so much was his message imbued with the idea of the presence of God amidst his own.

The Prophetic Whirlwind

Everything begins for Ezekiel with a kind of huge canvas which at the very least you would say was dizzying. A big cloud—which immediately makes you think of the sanctuary and the temple—tongues of fire; four living beings who are like other human beings

1. 2 Kgs 24:1–17.

and yet not like human beings; wheels of enormous diameter, with eyes all around them. And they turn in all directions, they go upwards, backwards all in the middle of a deafening noise. You do not get it? Me neither. Has the prophet somehow encompassed everything? Nothing could be further from the truth. When the story surfaces again in chapter 10, Ezekiel gives these wheels the name "whirlwind." An appropriate title if ever there was one. What is the meaning of this piece of heavenly engineering? It is very easy to get lost in the details in trying to understand the whole. Ezekiel puts us on the right track: "Like the bow in a cloud on a rainy day, such was the appearance of the splendor all around. This was the appearance of the likeness of the glory of the Lord. When I saw it, I fell on my face, and I heard the voice of someone speaking."[2] This heavenly spectacular, this perpetual motion is in a way quite simply the glory of the Lord. And when he understands that it is with the glory of the Lord that he has to do, the prophet falls down prostrate. A little further on, the glory of the Lord is tied up with the place where he lives,[3] the place where he shows himself. In other words we can say without a shadow of doubt that, in the book of Ezekiel, right from the beginning, the glory of the Lord is the sign of God's presence. There is no longer any temple in Jerusalem but God has not thereby become a person of "no fixed address." The Israelites had thought that God could not do without a temple: any destruction of the sacred place would jeopardize his existence. Big mistake. God persists. God is always there, very much so! He is the God without a temple, but his glory is much more important than the building built by Solomon. But what of this vision, frenzied, manic even where the words are so baffling? The young exiled priest, excluded forever from any temple, he understood. For him—no temple but simply and all-sufficiently—the presence of God.

Solomon had acknowledged in his inaugural prayer that the heavens could not contain the presence of God.[4] And of that

2. Ezek 1:26–28.
3. Ezek 3:12.
4. 1 Kgs 8:27.

breathtaking confirmation is given here to Ezekiel at the beginning of his book. Solomon had tried to confine God within four walls. It was a stupid thing to attempt. For here God rises, turns, left, right, twists forwards and backwards. God is restless. God is restless with love. It is impossible for his love to keep still. When you want to be with your own people it is best to be lithe and flexible. This astonishing display given in the vision has no parallel. Who after this would want to run the risk of shutting God up in a temple?

From Whirlwind to Desolation

God himself had adapted however. In a way he had agreed to become small in order to fill the temple of Solomon with his glory.[5] Now remember it did not take very long for Solomon—quickly followed by a number of his successors—to create other sacred spaces for foreign deities. Jerusalem became a kind of religious hypermarket, a big department store where if the customer is not satisfied with what he finds in one aisle can go to the next. But God accepts no competition. He regards any competition as unfair. Crucially he knows that what is on offer is a vast deception purveyed by the greatest trickster, liar, and swindler of all time. He asks Ezekiel to go public with his decision. He is shutting up shop in Jerusalem. He will leave the people to their own devices.

Quite simply Jerusalem is worse than all the other towns. Worse than Sodom, worse than Samaria.[6] Jerusalem is so bad—a prostitute—that God can no longer bare to be in the same place with her.[7] As for the people themselves, they have not budged an inch since Egypt: always the same, they have not given up on their idols.[8] So God says: "I'm off."

Can that really be so? God will show himself more comfortable with coming back than with leaving. In the airports or the

5. 1 Kgs 8:11.
6. Ezek 16:44–58.
7. Ezek 16:15–43.
8. Ezek 20:8–12.

stations of our lives he prefers—by a very great margin—the arrivals hall to departures. He prefers those outlines of life which more or less make sense. I hate railway platforms, trains slowly pulling away, and hands waving to us from the other side of the window, moist eyes. When God has no choice but to leave he always has a return ticket in his pocket. In the Bible it is called a promise.

The Temple? God Is the Temple

God promises Ezekiel a return to the promised land, with another temple:

> Therefore say: Thus says the Lord God: Though I removed them far away among the nations, and though I scattered them among the countries, yet I have been a sanctuary to them for a little while in the countries where they have gone. Therefore say: Thus says the Lord God: I will gather you from the peoples, and assemble you out of the countries where you have been scattered, and I will give you the land of Israel. When they come there, they will remove from it all its detestable things and all its abominations. I will give them one heart, and put a new spirit within them; I will remove the heart of stone from their flesh and give them a heart of flesh, so that they may follow my statutes and keep my ordinances and obey them. Then they shall be my people, and I will be their God. But as for those whose heart goes after their detestable things and their abominations, I will bring their deeds upon their own heads, says the Lord God.[9]

When there is no longer any sacred dwelling, God himself becomes that dwelling-place. During this period of captivity when there is no temple in Jerusalem, when there is no replacement temple in Babylon, God gives this reassurance to his people: "I am your temple." In other words God says: "In spite of all these trials, rest assured that I will remain in your midst. I do not need a space enclosed by four walls and a roof to show that I am there." It is

---

9. Ezek 11:16–21.

an amazing thing to say, a drastic step to make the holy space—the temple—disappear so that the divine presence could appear. In fact it is a repetition of the message addressed to David: God does not want him to build a house, but he is going to build a structure which will last forever, a royal household. God repeats in no uncertain terms that it is not a permanent structure which he is interested in, no "house" is needed because he is the temple. If you cannot grasp this teaching then you will have great difficulty in understanding the New Testament.

But is this the end of all building of holy spaces? Not at all. The end of the book of Ezekiel is devoted entirely to a new temple. But not one like that which already exists. A temple yes but quite different.

The Vision of Another Temple

Ezekiel devotes no less than eight chapters to the description of the new temple. The prophet is perched on a very high mountain. A man with a look of bronze about him tells him to look and listen.[10] Ezekiel is about to witness a great sound and light show.

Everything is described in minute detail: the suite of rooms, the inside of the temple itself, the auxiliary buildings, the perimeter fence, the altar, the kitchens. And in addition the conditions for getting in, and the rules for the different holy days.[11] It is chapter 47 which particularly attracts my attention. We are a long way away here from the expected descriptions where the abundance of details often overwhelms the modern reader.

Ezekiel has finished his description. But the holy dwelling seems to be flawed by a building defect. Warning! There is a water leak in the basement. Was the architect unaware of the problem? Whatever the case the whole place has been built over a spring that generates an underground stream. It runs along one side of the building. It is about ten centimeters at the beginning. Another

10. Ezek 40:4.
11. See Ezek 40–47.

five hundred meters further along, it has reached a depth of a meter, then one and a half meters five hundred meters further along. Then more than two meters in less than two kilometers. At this point it is a torrent that no one can cross.

Ezekiel is taken to the river's edge. Many trees line the edge of the water which plunges down southwards towards what is called the Dead Sea.

And plunging is the right word. The watercourse which had its source on Mount Zion, nine hundred meters high, spills out into the Dead Sea, the lowest point on earth at four hundred meters below sea level. That is a drop of about one thousand two hundred meters in thirty kilometers. The torrent follows is whimsical but not destructive in nature. It lacks the sort of abrasive power which would erode its banks. On the contrary it is a source of life along its length. It gives rise to luxuriant vegetation: all sorts of fruit trees whose foliage is forever green, which gives fruit every month, and which have healing properties. When the torrent reaches its final destination, the sea of death, it purifies the water. This place which was the despair of fishermen because there was not the slightest sign of life in it—no trace of fish or shellfish—now becomes a sea with pure water, rich in all kinds of animal life like the Mediterranean.

Any pilgrim-tourists who have been able to visit these places and who have made the journey from Jerusalem to the Dead Sea can well visualize what is described here. For between the point of departure (Mount Zion) and the point of arrival (the shores of the Dead Sea) the landscape is just desert, arid and inhospitable as far as the eye can see. You dare not stop, you go down like a descent into hell. And when you arrive way below, often in a suffocating heat, you cannot even benefit from a refreshing dip in the sea, because it is so uninviting. Of course tourists pose for the usual photo where you sit reading your newspaper sitting in the sea, kept afloat by the salt which will quickly remind anyone tempted to linger of its extraordinary density. Dead Sea—dead in name and dead in nature.

But let us now imagine the same places after the vision of Ezekiel. Desert no more but rich vegetation. Date palms, palm trees, and all sorts of fruit trees. Below a good restaurant serving fish—fish fresh from clear, unpolluted waters. Before the meal a refreshing swim in water at an ideal temperature (twenty-six degrees Celsius). Paradise!

Yes paradise indeed because the description given by Ezekiel has a strong scent of the garden of Eden. It reminds us of the fourth itinerary devoted to the symbolism of the sanctuary and of the temple. Every capital must have a temple. Every temple is the center of the world in habited by God. Every moment of absence from the temple matches the desert places from which God is absent. When he left the temple in Jerusalem, God made Jerusalem into a desert, a place of death. But when he returns hell becomes paradise again. Even that sea which is Dead becomes a fertile place again, a place of superabundance. Health and happiness are in the air. Everything flows from the temple, from this small watercourse that no one can cross, like this small stone which sculpts itself without the aid of any human hand and which is the symbol of the kingdom of God.[12]

When Ezekiel surfaces from his vision, from this extravagant multimedia show to which he had been transported, he is very clear that his God is one who longs to be among his people. Not shut up between four walls in some holy palace, but like a torrent which no-one can control, which transforms deserts into fertile land, which changes salty, dirty, polluted water into sea which is alive; a God who feeds, waters, cares.

Certain texts in the Old Testament are couched in technical terms. They are called prototypes of the Gospel. I have never read that this chapter of Ezekiel falls in this category. But it thoroughly deserves to be classified thus. For this temple, that is the presence of God among his own people, or the little stream which comes from beneath Mount Zion, this is the best news ever.

---

12. Dan 2:44ff.

Interlude

It is time to pause for a moment. Just to do a tour of the different Jewish temples which are linked directly or indirectly with biblical history. For there were other temples built beside that in Jerusalem.

Temples in Bible Lands

The Temple of Solomon

- Also called the first temple.
- Inaugurated in 959 BCE.
- Destroyed in 587/6 by the army of Nebuchadnezzar.
- No significant archaeological remains of this first temple survive.

The Temple of Zerrubabel

- Also known as the second temple.
- Proportions more modest than the first (see Hag 2:3; Ezra 3:12).
- Inaugurated in 515 BCE.

- Desecrated by Antiochus Epiphanes IV in 169 BCE. Here is the description of this desecration as found in the first book of Maccabees:

  > After subduing Egypt, Antiochus returned in the one hundred forty-third year. He went up against Israel and came to Jerusalem with a strong force. He arrogantly entered the sanctuary and took the golden altar, the lampstand for the light, and all its utensils. He took also the table for the bread of the Presence, the cups for drink offerings, the bowls, the golden censers, the curtain, the crowns, and the gold decoration on the front of the temple; he stripped it all off. He took the silver and the gold, and the costly vessels; he took also the hidden treasures that he found. Taking them all, he went into his own land.
  > He shed much blood,
  > and spoke with great arrogance.
  > Israel mourned deeply in every community,
  > rulers and elders groaned,
  > young women and young men became faint,
  > the beauty of the women faded.
  > Every bridegroom took up the lament;
  > she who sat in the bridal chamber was mourning.
  > Even the land trembled for its inhabitants,
  > and all the house of Jacob was clothed with shame.[1]

- Antiochus dedicates this temple to Zeus (1 Macc 6:1,11).
- Purified and restored in 164 after a war lasting six years, led most notably by Judas Maccabeus.

The Samaritan Temple

- Built on top of Mount Gerizim, the mountain sacred to the Samaritans, probably around the fifth century BCE, to rival the temple of Zerrubabel.

---

1. 1 Macc 1:20–28.

- Existence confirmed by Flavius Josephus.[2]
- Desecrated and dedicated to Zeus the Hospitaller by Antiochus Epiphanes IV.[3]
- Destroyed by John Hyrcan, high priest in Jerusalem in 128 BCE.[4]
- This act of destruction largely explains the hostility between the Jews and Samaritans.
- The Samaritan women whom Jesus met is certainly making reference to this temple.[5]

Herod's Temple

- From 20 BCE Herod the Great starts to enlarge the second temple.
- The works will last until 64 CE.
- This is the temple known and visited by Jesus and the first Christians.
- Flavius Josephus indicates that construction works never interrupted worship.[6]
- Temple burned down in 70 CE by Roman troops under Titus.

Contrary to current opinion it is by no means certain that this fire marked the end of the temple. It was not the first time that the temple had been damaged or desecrated. Why would the Jews have concluded in 70 CE that this fire marked the bitter end? There is evidence to show that once the trauma of the fire and the accompanying massacre had passed, certain of the faithful went

---

2. Josephus, *Ant.* 11.310.
3. 2 Macc 6:2.
4. Josephus, *Ant.* 13.254–56.
5. John 4:20.
6. Josephus, *Ant.* 14.380–425; *J.W.* 5:184–237.

up routinely on to the dais to offer some sacrifices and to celebrate the major feasts.[7]

The Temple of Bar Kokhba

During the second Jewish war (132–135 CE) Herod's Temple was probably partially restored by the pretender Bar Kokhba. Certain coins from the period were minted bearing his image.

Irritated by these religious stirrings with their political undertones, the Emperor Hadrian had the esplanade ploughed up with the furrowing removing all signs of the foundations of Herod's temple. With all sign of the exact location of the holy places gone, no Jew would risk going up on to the esplanade of the temple for fear of walking on the site of the most holy place.

Israelite Temples in Egypt

The Elephantine Temple

- Temple of the Jewish community composed largely of soldiers and their families, built on the Elephantine Island in Egypt, near the modern city of Asswan. These soldiers were responsible for protecting the southern border of Egypt. They had probably been sent by King Manasseh in support of the pharaoh Psammetichus in the struggles with the Nubians.
- Erected about 600 BCE.
- Destroyed in 410 BCE by the priests of the Egyptian god Khnoum who would not tolerate any competition from another temple on such a small island.
- The Jewish colony sought the backing of the Jerusalemites to rebuild it but without success.

---

7. Clark, "Worship in the Jerusalem Temple," 269–80.

- Regular practice of the main sacrifices: animal sacrifices, incense offering, vegetable offerings.[8]
- In order to avoid the Judean sanction which did not permit any other temple than that in Jerusalem, this temple was dedicated to YHW and not to YHWH, with the Tetragram (the name of God in Hebrew) shortened by one letter.
- A letter sent by the leaders of the temple in Jerusalem required the Jewish Elephantine community to observe the same calendar as in Israel for Passover.

The Temple of Leontopolis

- Situated at Leontopolis, thirty kilometers north of Cairo.
- Built for the use of the Jewish colony established by the high priest Onias IV, who had fled Jerusalem in 165 BCE and seen his pre-eminent sacrificial role lost to him.
- Built to the same specifications as the temple in Jerusalem. Onias claimed to be fulfilling the prophecy of Isaiah which had foretold the existence of an altar to the Lord in Egypt.[9]
- In use until 73 CE when Vespasian ordered its closure.

The Temples of the Essenes

From the first century BCE three groups made up Judaism: the Pharisees, the Sadducees, and the Essenes. The Essenes were made famous by the discovery of the Dead Sea Scrolls at Qumran from 1947. The link between the Qumran caves and the Essenes is well attested though it remains a topic for debate among certain specialists. The many manuscripts and other fragments excavated in different caves have a clear provenance in the Essene community which settled here. We know today that the Essenes did not confine

---

8. Porten and Yardeni, *Textbook of Aramaic*, vol. 1, Letters 7.20–27.
9. Porten, Farben, Marin, and Vittmann, *Passover Letter*, 126–27.

themselves to living in a community isolated from the world. A good number of them lived in a district of Jerusalem not far from the temple.

The theme of the temple appears frequently in manuscripts typically produced by the Essenes. The longest scroll found at Qumran, which is eight meters long, is called the *Temple Scroll*.[10] It gave a very detailed description of the temple which was to be built to replace the Temple in Jerusalem now considered to be tarnished and corrupted. The description of the building derives from the book of Exodus. This temple, restored and cleansed, must correspond to the one God showed Moses on the mountain. But this temple is not permanent. It will be the business of the Messiah to build the ultimate temple.[11]

---

10. 1QS19.

11. 4Q174, I, 1–7 (4Q*Florilegium*). See also *Jub.* 1:15–17 and *1 En.* 90:29 which, though not belonging *per se* to the Essenian library are very close to it. They predict the building of a new temple.

PART 2

Prologue

It is customary when one turns to the New Testament to follow the order of the Canon. Thus, in our search for God's dwelling among his people, the common practice would be to start considering first the gospels, and then the letters. For our topic, as for any other study, I do not believe that this order is the most helpful. For it must be remembered that most of the letters of the New Testament were written before the Synoptic Gospels (Matthew, Mark and Luke). Paul never quotes the gospels, which tends to prove that he did not have yet a written edition available. Regarding the letters, they were all written before the temple went up in flames in 70 CE. There is no doubt that the events described in the gospels predate those reported in the letters, but they were written after the letters. These letters were written about the same time as the events they record and interpret. By contrast, for the gospels, oral traditions concerning Jesus circulated hither and yon for several decades before the authors put them into a written form. This lapse of time was by no means without its benefits. It provided an opportunity for reinterpretations and finally deepening of understanding. We will therefore turn first towards Paul's letters before considering the Synoptic Gospels.

ITINERARY 1

God's House in Paul's Letters
or, When God Moves On

Paul and the Temple: Biographical Notes

EVEN THOUGH PAUL TRIES very hard to present himself as an eighteen-carat-gold Jew, "a Jew, born in Tarsus in Cilicia, but brought up in this city at the feet of Gamaliel, educated strictly according to our ancestral law,"[1] the temple is not really his thing. By that I mean that we do not find him there very often, unlike the early Christians who were in regular attendance there. One episode confirms our suspicion that going to the temple was not for him a natural instinct.[2]

On returning from his third missionary journey, Paul returns to Jerusalem. His missionary report—and what a missionary report it was—aroused enthusiasm and fear in equal measure among the church authorities in Jerusalem. For the remarkable success of Paul generated hostility and rumor: Paul wished to draw the Jews away from Moses, he would abolish circumcision and demand that that ancient customs no longer be followed. In order to put an end to such poisonous talk, Paul is advised to go into the temple

1. See Acts 22:3.
2. See Acts 21:15–36.

with four faithful brethren who have taken vow, to purify himself, to pay for them the sum of money which they were obliged to give, everything necessary to show the people that he has nothing against the house of God in Jerusalem. Paul complies fully. But political correctness, particularly when it has to do with religion rarely pays off. He is wrongly accused of having entered the temple with non-Jews. He is immediately arrested and dragged outside the holy precincts. Poor Paul! The one time he goes to Mount Zion he is arrested and summoned to explain himself.

Paul goes on to tell the story of his conversion. Luke includes in his account a significant detail given the context. It is while he is praying in the temple that Paul goes into vision and hears the voice of God telling him to turn his missionary efforts towards non-Jews.[3] Paul tries hard to argue his case. He tries to insist that he is without sin in any respect, having "in no way committed an offense against the law of the Jews, or against the temple, or against the emperor,"[4] but to no effect. Alas the accusation against him is heard: "He even tried to profane the temple"[5] was the chorus of his accusers, high priest Ananias, certain of the elders and their lawyer Tertullus. It is a strange irony: Paul himself no lover of the temple is in the end arrested because of the temple. If I were making the case against him I would have definitely found some better arguments of the following kind: "This man insists that salvation is free regardless of any observance of the law." But no, it is the allegedly defiled temple which brings about Paul's downfall. Does that remind you of another story?

Paul and the Temple: Questions of Language

It is obviously the case that Paul does not go up to the temple every day. How could he? He is spending most of his time crisscrossing the Mediterranean basin to preach the gospel. But that does not

---

3. Acts 22:17–21.
4. Acts 25:8.
5. Acts 24:6.

mean that ideas of the temple, of the house of God, of his dwelling place are foreign to him. We must pause here to analyze his writings in order to establish the extent of the semantic domains of "building" and "construction" in order to make appropriate comparisons with Old Testament quotations which make reference to the theme of the temple and the sanctuary.[6]

Quotations and References

Paul is entirely familiar with the desert experience endured by his ancestors. But he only makes two references to it. The first time in rather dark terms to recall that "God was not pleased with most of them, and they were struck down in the wilderness."[7] The second time in reference to Moses whose face shines with a dazzling light when he comes down from Sinai.[8]

Paul never makes mention of the building of the wilderness sanctuary as described in the book of Exodus, nor of David's project to build a house for the Lord, nor of God's reply promising him that there would always be one of his descendants on his throne. He says nothing of the building of the temple in Jerusalem, nor of its final reconstruction, nothing about its decoration or the numerous setbacks along the way. Solomon receives no mention at all.

Cloud and Glory

We have seen that both "cloud" and "glory" play an important role in the Old Testament to indicate the divine presence. Paul only mentions "cloud" once.[9] He uses the word "glory" extensively—more

---

6. See Louw and Nida, *Greek English Lexicon*. According to these authors, there are ninety-three semantic domains in the New Testament. Words such as house, habitation, temple, sanctuary, and tent belong to the domain of constructions, and the subdomain of buildings.

7. 1 Cor 10:5.

8. 2 Cor 3:7.

9. 1 Cor 10:1–2.

than eighty times in all. But in his writing this word never refers to the visible presence in a particular place.

Tent—Sanctuary—Temple

In the style of Greek writers, Paul uses the word "tent" not for one or other part of the sanctuary but to denote the human body, as in the following text: "For we know that if the earthly tent we live in is destroyed, we have a building from God, a house not made with hands, eternal in the heavens."[10]

Paul does not use the word "sanctuary" or any of its synonyms. But he uses the word "temple" a dozen times, twice to refer to a pagan temple[11] and once to describe the action of the Lawless One who occupies the temple and proclaims himself God.[12] As for the other occurrences, they are all fundamentally important because they all register a very significant change of meaning employed by the great apostle.

In an early passage, the word "temple" refers to the human body which is the temple of the Holy Spirit: "Or do you not know that your body is a temple of the Holy Spirit within you, which you have from God, and that you are not your own? For you were bought with a price; therefore glorify God in your body."[13]

Two parallel passages point in an entirely different direction where the "temple" means the community of believers. The first is in 1 Corinthians: "Do you not know that you are God's temple and that God's Spirit dwells in you? If anyone destroys God's temple, God will destroy that person. For God's temple is holy, and you are that temple."[14] The second is in 2 Corinthians:

> Do not be mismatched with unbelievers. For what partnership is there between righteousness and lawlessness?

---

10. 2 Cor 5:1.
11. Rom 2:22; 1 Cor 8:10.
12. 2 Thess 2:3–4.
13. 1 Cor 6:19–20.
14. 1 Cor 3:16–17.

Or what fellowship is there between light and darkness?
What agreement does Christ have with Beliar? Or what does a believer share with an unbeliever? What agreement has the temple of God with idols? For we are the temple of the living God; as God said,

"I will live in them and walk among them,

and I will be their God,

and they shall be my people.

Therefore come out from them,

and be separate from them, says the Lord,

and touch nothing unclean;

then I will welcome you,

and I will be your father,

and you shall be my sons and daughters,

says the Lord Almighty."[15]

This constitutes a radical change in biblical thought, which indicates clearly that Paul does not conceive of the temple as a building or any place in which God lives. These texts deserve special attention.

The Temple—The Community of Believers

What is it that drives Paul to innovate? What are the underlying reasons for this new understanding of the temple of God? In other words what do we know of the context in Corinth which can support and enlarge our understanding?

Corinth, it is the Beirut of the Ancient world! Bullets are flying in all directions without our quite knowing where they are coming from and who fired them. It is disorder, confusion, a mess, and complete chaos. The letters of Paul themselves show signs of this state of affairs. Are there only two letters? Or three? What of the letter "written in tears"? The connections are often very abrupt. One theme follows another often without it being easy to find any connection. But whatever the reasons, it is clear to us that

15. 2 Cor 6:14–18.

worrying news has reached Paul about the situation in Corinth. It is clear that certain questions have been put to him by some of the believers concerning some specific problems in the community. It is clear that he has replied to them.

One of the problems in Corinth comes down to a struggle between factions. The church is divided into at least three groups: on one side are those who claim to be followers of Apollos, on another those who are for Paul himself, and another group identify with Cephas.[16] One group is faithful to the one who first proclaimed the gospel to them—Paul. Another mongrel group interbreed the faith of the fathers with the riches of the Hellenistic world—Apollos is their mastermind. Yet another group is fiercely loyalist, prizes above all its ties with the mother church—Jerusalem—and the founding fathers—Peter the central column—and is undoubtedly the measure of reliability and truth. The stakes are not entirely theological. The truth and purity of doctrine are not the issue. But between these different groups are endless disputes and corrosive jealousies that put the whole community at risk.

Paul replies using a double metaphor: the first uses the language of gardening and the second of building.[17]

Gardening Metaphor

- Paul plants;
- Apollos waters;
- But God alone gives growth;
- Planting and watering are one and the same;
- Everyone involved is God's helper.

---

16. 1 Cor 1:12.
17. 1 Cor 3:5–9; 1 Cor 3:10–15.

Building Metaphor

- Paul is the site manager;
- Paul lays the foundations;
- Someone else builds on these foundations;
- Jesus Christ is the one foundation;
- All kinds of different materials are used.

The quality of the building materials and the skill of the workers will be subject to the test of time.

These two metaphors have three ideas in common. Paul always appears first in them. He is the original planter or the site manager. Then one single worker cannot achieve the project. One always needs several coworkers or several types of material. Last, God calls the tune. He alone is the one who produces growth. Who could quarrel with that? There is one detail which we should note. The reference to Jesus Christ as the only possible foundation has negative connotations: "For no one can lay any foundation other than the one that has been laid; that foundation is Jesus Christ."[18] Was there someone in Corinth who would dare to suggest another foundation? This is more than likely. The rest of the text seems to confirm this suspicion: "If you think that you are wise in this age, you should become fools so that you may become wise."[19] The deep roots of the crisis lie simply in this: someone has a big head. Are you looking for a name? Well I am not going to give you one, at least not for the time being.

There is someone who takes themselves as the foundation stone. Someone who has forgotten that in building, there is only one Lord who can lay this stone, as Isaiah says: "See, I am laying in Zion a foundation stone, a tested stone, a precious cornerstone, a sure foundation: 'One who trusts will not panic.'"[20]

---

18. 1 Cor 3:11.
19. 1 Cor 3:18.
20. Isa 28:16.

"If anyone destroys God's temple, God will destroy that person."[21] So you, whoever you are, just be careful! You are looking to take the number one spot for yourself. You would have everyone believe that, without you, the community in Corinth would not exist. You believe yourself to be the most important one, no, the only one. So you, whoever you are, are playing a dangerous game. Dangerous for this reason: the community of faith is not a list of names on a register, not rows of seats or benches in more or less comfortable premises. The community of faith in Corinth—any community of faith wherever it may be—is nothing less than the house of God, the temple in which he has chosen to live. Not a building made of cement, plaster and wooden beams, but a building made of human beings. Made of human mortar, you whoever you are, just human mortar! You cannot play with human mortar because this human mortar is now home to God. It is the temple, no more, no less. If you meddle with these human beings who are building community, you meddle with the temple of God. Do not for one moment believe that God will let it pass.

A name, a name! A scapegoat who will focus in himself alone this evil endemic in many Christian communities today. It is very useful to have a scapegoat. Useful but rarely enough. The sin of being a big head is not listed among the Ten Commandments. And yet how many churches today suffer from the Corinthian syndrome. A name, a name! Many names, all the names of we who, by our ambitions, our frustrations, our career paths, our pride, debase and finally destroy the temple of God. No better than Nebuchadnezzar. No better than Antiochus Epiphanes, at the time of the Maccabees. No better than Titus or any of the others.

After the repeated and painful collapse of the temple building—and don't forget the worst is yet to come for Herod's temple is still standing when Paul writes these lines—God confirms that he wants to invest not in stone but in humans. God is moving house. In fact God is completely relocating. Whenever two or three meet together, he will be there, in his temple. But on the clear understanding that Jesus Christ be laid as the only foundation. The

---

21. 1 Cor 3:17.

crowds, the meetings, the communities, be they spiritual or religious, are not temples of God, not places where he lives. And to be quite sure it is necessary to go down to the basement in order to check the state of the foundations. Sand or rock? In this world which is not his kingdom, shaken by storms and all kinds of disasters, God has planned a building which recognizes seismic laws: dressed stone as the only foundation. His son. The promise made to David is honored. God himself builds the house. And he invites human beings to come and live in it. Does that mean all human beings? Here is Paul's answer to that question:

> Do not be mismatched with unbelievers. For what partnership is there between righteousness and lawlessness? Or what fellowship is there between light and darkness? What agreement does Christ have with Beliar? Or what does a believer share with an unbeliever? What agreement has the temple of God with idols? For we are the temple of the living God; as God said,
> I will live in them and walk among them,
> and I will be their God,
> and they shall be my people.
> Therefore come out from them,
> and be separate from them, says the Lord,
> and touch nothing unclean;
> then I will welcome you,
> and I will be your father,
> and you shall be my sons and daughters,
> says the Lord Almighty.[22]

One of the purposes of the temple was to define a sacred space. The temple was the house of God, the place of purity over against the wider world which is the place of impurity. The rites by which the believer gained access to the temple were just as much about allowing him to move from impurity to purity and finally to divinity. When all is said and done the worshipper had no other means than via the priests who played the essential role

22. 2 Cor 6:14–18.

of go-between. If the new temple was the community of believers then there could be no question of turning it into a den of thieves. The unbelievers were outside. This was no place for those who did not believe, for idolaters. Do you remember the famous story of the king with two lovers who built at virtually the same time one temple for God and other temples for idols? Yes Solomon himself. In the new temple / community of believers, adulterers are not admitted. Nor rebellious children. Cohabitation—especially with God—is not their thing.

So God has moved house, says Paul to the Corinthians. God, the great banker of the universe, has moved his investments. From bricks and mortar he has moved into human resources. Actually it is a return to his roots for he has always had a preference for investing in human beings, but for a while he has had to bow to the demands of the market—human free will. So it is going back to human mortar. But he does not content himself with simply residing in the midst of the faithful.

The Temple—The Body

So we move from the community to the personal level of the individual. The Corinthian context encourages another development where the idea of the temple as the residence of God takes on still another meaning. In Corinth it is in fact not only internal tensions in the community which cause the problems. In addition it is the individual behavior of some of his members in the wider society. For certain Corinthians are quick to distort Paul's thinking. Did he not say, "All things are lawful for me"?[23] If everything is lawful . . . well, it is a chance to have a bonanza! It is a phrase that can produce devastating effects if picked up by immature minds and adolescent thinkers. And that is exactly what these Corinthians are: they think they know everything but in fact they are "infants."[24] It

---

23. 1 Cor 6:12.
24. 1 Cor 3:1–3.

is perhaps not surprising that they are a little pretentious, after all Corinth is not just any old town.

Corinth was a new city of about five hundred thousand inhabitants. A Greek city with a population embracing all sorts of ethnic groups; different religions practicing oriental forms of worship; endless temples and sanctuaries; burgeoning commercial activity thanks to its port with access to the Aegean and the Adriatic; but at the same time some real social tensions between the rich elite and the many poor. The decline in morals, which some commentators get very excited about, certainly existed, the practice of sacred prostitution being an example, but it was no different from any other large city in the region at that time. The population was by no means easy to manage. The church was a mirror of the surrounding syncretism, where all ideas and beliefs became muddled together, and was a place where it was difficult to exercise any kind of authority. In the midst of all this Paul explains his expression "everything is lawful."

> All things are lawful for me, but not all things are beneficial. "All things are lawful for me," but I will not be dominated by anything. "Food is meant for the stomach and the stomach for food," and God will destroy both one and the other. The body is meant not for fornication but for the Lord, and the Lord for the body. And God raised the Lord and will also raise us by his power. Do you not know that your bodies are members of Christ? Should I therefore take the members of Christ and make them members of a prostitute? Never! Do you not know that whoever is united to a prostitute becomes one body with her? For it is said, "The two shall be one flesh." But anyone united to the Lord becomes one spirit with him. Shun fornication! Every sin that a person commits is outside the body; but the fornicator sins against the body itself. Or do you not know that your body is a temple of the Holy Spirit within you, which you have from God, and that you are not your own? For you were bought with a price; therefore glorify God in your body.[25]

---

25. 1 Cor 6:12–20.

The theme of belonging runs through the paragraph. It is the key to unlocking the whole argument that resolves itself into one question: to whom do you belong?

- I will not let myself be mastered by anything (v. 12);
- You are not your own (v. 19);
- For someone has paid the price of your freedom (v. 20).

Where is this idea of "belonging" played out? At the level of the body—the word is used eight times. Three rhetorical questions summarize the teaching of Paul:

- Do you not know that your bodies are members of Christ (v. 15)?
- Do you not know that he who unites himself with a prostitute is one with her in body (v. 16)?
- Do you not know that your body is the temple of the Holy Spirit (v. 19)?

No you do not know. But you should know! You should know that the body is not to be neglected. The evidence? That it is the body which is resurrected.[26] You should know that your body which is so personal to you actually is part of something which transcends it: your body is a member of Christ. Through your body you are, every one of you, in some way grafted into Christ. You should know that your body shelters, gives hospitality to divinity. You do not *go* to the temple. You do not go up to the temple to meet God. The Holy Spirit settles in your body and makes his temple there. When you look at the text carefully, you see that all the signs of divinity are implied in this unheard act of occupation:

- The Lord God is for the body and resurrects it (vv. 13, 14);
- The body is a member of Christ (v. 15);
- The body is the temple of the Holy Spirit (v. 19).

---

26. The resurrection was quite a difficult topic for the early Christians—and not only for them. Paul will address it again, with mastery, in 1 Cor 15.

So from then on is it worth bothering with prostitution? Promiscuous love once more is at the heart of the text. The believer who lives in his body under the same roof as the Holy Spirit, who is occupied by the Holy Spirit, who welcomes the Holy Spirit cannot in any way contemplate this sort of promiscuity. The temple is small, only big enough for a couple, not for a threesome.

The temple is small but what a temple! The Corinthians were prepared to listen to anything and everything but not that their body had the rank and status of a divine dwelling place, these people for whom wisdom and knowledge were above all else. It is these highly cerebral Corinthians that Paul has to get to understand that "the wisdom of this world is foolishness with God"[27] that a certain type of knowledge "puffs (us) up,"[28] that it is entirely limited and destined for the scrap heap.[29] All of Paul's "do you not knows" must have sounded very odd to the ears of these Corinthians who claimed to know everything, and who claimed quite wrongly that their knowledge was the engine of their existence, to the total exclusion of their body. There were several effects of this exclusive emphasis on the cerebral: on the one hand, a life of unbridled debauchery as an expression of one's freedom, on the other, a rigid asceticism in which any sexual activity was unthinkable. On the one hand the "everything is permitted" is pushed to its limits, prostitution included. On the other hand, there come all the questions on marriage, on celibacy, and on sexuality which are the subject of the following chapter in the first letter to the Corinthians.

Among the must-see places on any visit to Jerusalem is the temple esplanade, the "Mount of the House" as the Hebrew has it. That is where all the temples stood, from Solomon to Herod and Bar Kokhba. The pilgrim traveller cannot miss this warning sign above the entrance gate, quoted here *verbatim*:

---

27. 1 Cor 3:18.
28. 1 Cor 8:1.
29. 1 Cor 13:8.

> NOTICE AND WARNING
> ENTRANCE TO THE AREA OF THE TEMPLE MOUNT
> IS FORBIDDEN TO EVERYONE BY JEWISH LAW
> OWING TO THE SACREDNESS OF THE PLACE
> THE CHIEF RABBINATE OF ISRAEL

The place is holy. It must be kept from any blemish. After having read the First Letter of Paul to the Corinthians, it would clearly be obligatory to take down from the enclosure wall of what today is called the mosque esplanade this warning sign. It should rather be put up in the middle of any community of faith. Warning: holy ground, for you are the temple of God. At the same time it is a sign to be attached to the human body, for it would undoubtedly be a strong incentive to follow a Christian ethic in life. Warning: holy ground. The Holy Spirit abides here.

ITINERARY 2

Mark and the Temple of God
The Torn Curtain

LET'S BEGIN BY REMINDING ourselves of a few general characteristics so that we can understand the gospels properly:

- The gospels of Matthew, Mark and Luke are called "synoptic" because they offer us roughly similar pictures of the life of Jesus.
- The Gospel of John presents a quite different account.
- Before taking on the written form that we are familiar with, the gospels were circulated orally.
- The business of setting down the gospels in writing took place about forty years after the events which they record in the case of the Synoptics, and about sixty years in the case of the Gospel of John.
- All of the gospels were written after the fire in the temple in Jerusalem in 70 CE.
- Although they often refer to the same events, the gospels must not be considered as four pieces of the same jigsaw that the reader must put together in order to have a comprehensive view. Each gospel contains its own truth, full and complete,

with its own understanding of the life of Jesus of Nazareth. The Holy Spirit did not distribute inspiration into four more or less equal parts between the evangelists, here a little, there a little. Each of the four authors is fully inspired.

- If the reader is inclined to compare the gospels (particularly the Synoptics) it must never be to superimpose one on another, to fill in gaps in Matthew by reference to Luke or John with Mark. The differences between them are much more significant and eloquent than their similarities.

- From a technical point of view it is widely agreed today that Mark was the first gospel to take on a written form, followed by Matthew and Luke. John follows towards the end of the first century. It is logical then to begin our investigation with Mark.

The Purified Temple: Mark 11

Let's start then with figs and a sandwich—a literary sandwich not meant to be eaten. The word "sandwich" here indicates a technique of literary composition used by Mark. Thus the account of the banishing of the traders from the temple is preceded by the story of the fig tree bearing no figs, and followed by a request for an explanation from Peter: "Rabbi, look! The fig tree that you cursed has withered."[1] The episode in the temple is set between the two references to the fig tree. These three paragraphs must not be understood and interpreted in isolation from each other because they form an indivisible whole, where each section illuminates the other and is in turn illuminated by the other.

In the journey which leads Jesus towards Jerusalem, Mark, who is well-known for his direct, no-frills style, mentions two villages, Bethpage and Bethany, without our seeing immediately why. Is Mark giving us a little (large, even) wink? Bethpage means in Aramaic "the house of figs." Bethany, the place where the anonymous woman will anoint the body of Jesus for his burial, is the first

1. Mark 11:21.

place where the good news will be proclaimed,[2] in advance. These are small but significant pauses on the road which leads to the cross.

From the opening of chapter 11, events seem to be out of sync. When he enters Jerusalem, Jesus goes towards the temple. But he is late. All he can do is take in the whole scene there and leave to return to Bethany. Is he overcome by tiredness? The next morning it seems that he has not taken time for a proper breakfast. After he leaves Bethany and finds the fig tree, it is not fatigue from the three kilometers he has walked which have exhausted him. It is hunger that makes him falter. Jesus decides that the timing mechanism of the fig tree is not set correctly. It should have borne some fruit even if it was not the season. Jesus accuses the tree of being out of sync, of showing the wrong time. Similarly, the Messiah has come. The crowds have given him an enthusiastic welcome: this was the very time for them to bear fruit. The fig tree did not want to or did not know how to synchronize itself with this important event. The episode in the temple goes on to clarify the meaning of all this.

This episode is clearly outlined: Jesus arrives in Jerusalem in the morning, after leaving Bethany. He leaves the city at nightfall.[3] Jerusalem is clearly not the resting place he prefers. He has chosen to live outside the city even though he was welcomed triumphantly as Messiah the day before. Mark takes only twenty lines to describe the scene that unfolds within the sacred precincts. But it undoubtedly took more time to happen than it takes to read about it. As he enters the temple, Jesus sets in motion the events which will make everything unravel.

Out with you buyers and sellers! It is not exactly clear what they were buying and selling, but the expression "den of thieves" which follows leaves us in little doubt that dishonest trade was taking place. The Temple Mount was a very busy place all day long, crowded not only with the inhabitants of Jerusalem but also with pilgrims from other parts of Palestine, with visiting Jews from the widely dispersed Jewish community, and with strangers. A remote

2. Mark 14:3–9.
3. Mark 11:15–19.

and desert place is rarely the preferred gathering place for merchants and all manner of hawkers and peddlers!

Out with you money changers! His grip on the situation is tightening. It is no longer just those who wish to do their deals, the sellers of souvenirs and other tacky trinkets. The money changers are a part of the religious apparatus. Roman currency is not legal tender in this holy place. Special temple coinage has been minted, to be used only in religious transactions. The faithful wishing to make an offering or an animal sacrifice have to use the money changers as agents in order to obtain the currency necessary for buying the animal they wanted to sacrifice. In effect worshipers have to pay an annual tax levied to subsidize the daily offerings in the temple. Without the money changers the temple simply cannot function.

Out with you sellers of doves! The story of the expulsion of the money changers and other merchants might have led some readers of the gospel to believe that it was only the wealthy who were responsible for the commotion in the temple. Some readers may have thought that it was the little people who were more pious and pure. That is not the case. In expelling the sellers of doves, Jesus recognizes that even the poorest worshippers may have had impure motives. It is important to remember that doves were the animals offered as a sacrifice by people with little money. So then it is the whole religious system of the temple that is undermined—at the very least—by Jesus.

All traffic is banned! "He would not allow anyone to carry anything through the temple."[4] Jesus turns himself here into a temple traffic policeman. You can well imagine him standing in the way of anyone wanting to use the temple court as a shortcut between the west of the city and the Mount of Olives, or between the lower part of the city in the south and the pool of Bethesda in the north. At this time four gates gave access to the temple: two to the south, one to the west and one to the east. You can imagine the news spreading quickly through the alleys of Jerusalem: "There is a guy blocking the way into the temple. You can't get through." You can imagine some smart operators trying to use another gate.

4. Mark 11:16.

One thing is sure; it would not have been easy for Jesus to direct the traffic in such a big space. And there were certainly none of his disciples to lend him a hand. The comings and goings in the alleyways were not going to be stopped in just a matter of minutes. Jesus spent a whole day on the esplanade. He did not confine himself to expelling them and banning them however.

"He was teaching and saying, is it not written, 'My house shall be called a house of prayer for all the nations'? But you have made it a den of robbers."[5]

Jesus did not simply tear things down and leave. He built things up with his teaching. Here again you cannot imagine that Jesus took only a few minutes to set things straight, to "reset the temple clock to the right time." Teaching involves repetition and more repetition. And these are not impressionable children that Jesus has before him, but a crowd deeply ingrained with traditional practices and fear of the religious authorities for whom the only acceptable change is reinforcement of the *status quo*. What a day for Jesus! Sellers chased out, tables of the money changers overturned, sellers of doves banished, all access blocked, teaching to persuade them of new things—by the end of the day, things were quieter: "the whole crowd was spellbound by his teaching."[6]

In the words of Isaiah that Jesus quotes, the tension between "the den of thieves" and the house of prayer for all nations is incredibly strong. It emphasizes the discrepancy between what has become of the temple in Jerusalem and what it was always meant to be. The exchange between Peter and Jesus on the fate of the fig tree that has become a dead skeleton of branches powerfully underscores the force of this quotation. In Jesus' explanation about what has happened, the word "prayer" appears twice, echoing his previous description of the temple as a place of prayer for all nations. Note that the prayer referred to here was prayer standing, the posture adopted by the priests and high priests officiating in the temple. Standing prayer was also a practice for all the faithful, a practice whose content and purpose were very specific: prayer

5. Mark 11:17, quoting Isa 56:7.
6. Mark 11:18.

for the pardon of sins. So in an instant our minds are returned to the temple. Prayer for forgiveness was a core raison d'être for that building and its sacrificial system. But instead of being a place of forgiveness, what had it become was nothing more than a great bazaar, a commercial center where the religious could peddle their wares, a hypermarket whose products succeeded only in poisoning the customer. Jesus appears here like a quality control officer to detect fraud. After the inspection, he announces the shutting down of the premises. The temple is dead just as the fig tree is shriveled. The forgiveness of sins has been moved from this venue. No need to turn up here any longer. Forgiveness is available to every standing believer-cum-priest, by faith alone. At this very moment, Jesus has just administered the fatal blow to this stunning building. The end of the temple, just like his own end, is near.

Toward Another Temple

When we have swallowed the literary sandwich of Mark, it is good to let our digestion follow its normal course that is to watch carefully the linking of paragraphs. Mark makes his connections. A temple makes way for another kind of place.

"Who do you think you are?"

There are no prizes for guessing that Jesus' comments about the fig tree and its relation with the temple did not arouse the same enthusiasm among the religious leaders as it had among the people. Jesus is not wearing temple uniform, nor an official badge to confer on him some authority or another. He is just like any other Jew in the public court. He knows very well that he has no license to do what he has done! So, when Jesus comes back to the temple and the authorities challenge him, he mischievously asks some embarrassing questions. He is certain of his ground: the high priests, scribes and elders have no answers.[7]

---

7. Mark 11:27–33.

Another Cornerstone

Since we are talking about temples and buildings, Jesus says, let's get back to basics. In chapter 12 of Mark, Jesus goes into parable mode so that only those who truly want to understand will get the point. The parable of the vine growers sets out clearly the story of the murder of the owner's son who has come to claim a share of the profits in proportion to his father's investment. From this picture of the world of viticulture, the text slips into a reference to the world of architecture. This change of register catches us unawares. Actually it is not a new connection in Jewish literature, where it is not unusual for the tower and the wine press to refer directly to the temple and the altar.[8]

"Have you not read this scripture: 'The stone that the builders rejected has become the cornerstone; this was the Lord's doing, and it is amazing in our eyes?'"[9]

You do not need a cornerstone among vines. But you do need a cornerstone in every type of construction, especially in a temple. But Jesus is not talking about an ordinary stone here. It is a stone of flesh, the only "stone" which is worth anything. The messianic stone: Jesus himself. Little by little the temple edifice is taking on quite another dimension, and it is not about architecture.

Love More Than Sacrifice

Even the scribes subscribed to the idea that the temple of stone should be replaced by a temple of flesh and blood. Is he serious, this scribe who comes to ask Jesus about the greatest of all the commandments? Jesus' reply confirms the shift: "Then the scribe said to him, 'You are right, Teacher; you have truly said that "he is one, and besides him there is no other"; and "to love him with all the heart, and with all the understanding, and with all the strength," and "to love one's neighbor as oneself,"—this is much more important than all whole burnt offerings and sacrifices.' When Jesus saw

8. See *1 En.* 99:50, 66, 67, 73; *Tg. Isa.* 5:1–7.
9. Mark 12:10–11.

that he answered wisely, he said to him, 'You are not far from the kingdom of God.'"[10] Although the scribe's reply is sound, he had probably not calculated the fall-out from it. If the burnt offerings and sacrifices become of secondary importance, what is the point of the temple?

The Temple Will Be Destroyed

The scribe has understood, in spite of himself probably. But not the disciples. They are still going into raptures about the building, that marble, those imperious columns, the architectural jewel crowning Mount Zion: "'Look, Teacher, what large stones and what large buildings!' Then Jesus asked him, 'Do you see these great buildings? Not one stone will be left here upon another; all will be thrown down.'"[11] Not one stone on another. Buildings leveled to the ground, here today gone tomorrow.

Another Temple Springs Up from Earth

The high priests and the whole Sanhedrin look for a leading witness against Jesus. Unable to find one they are forced to bribe some false witnesses. What credibility do they have? "We heard him say, 'I will destroy this temple that is made with hands, and in three days I will build another, not made with hands.' But even on this point their testimonies did not agree."[12] What a paradox! Those who have been bribed to tell lies actually tell the truth. Jesus does not respond to these accusations. For the real truth lies elsewhere. Another temple is coming for which there is no architect, no plans, no model. Now is not the time to speak of building. It is time to reveal his identity: "Jesus said, 'I am; and you will see the Son of Man seated at the right hand of the Power,' and 'coming with the clouds of heaven.'"[13]

10. Mark 12:32–34.
11. Mark 13:1–2.
12. Mark 14:58–59.
13. Mark 14:62.

The Veil Is Torn

So Jesus recognizes and proclaims that he is messiah. For the religious authorities there are no more need to resort to false witnesses. The dye is cast: out with this Messiah. Let him die! Spitting. Punching, slapping round the face.[14] In a few more hours the veil will be torn. The setting apart of sacred spaces will be irrelevant. No holy place, no most holy place, just an ordinary space. Access wide open to all, Jews and non-Jews without any sacrificial regime. Yes indeed, the stone once rejected has become the cornerstone of this house of prayer for all nations. God is still on the move. This time he leaves temple for good. He also leaves the tomb. Empty, both of them. He is no longer here. He is no longer there either. For the chief cornerstone cannot be confined inside any space.

---

14. Mark 14:65.

Itinerary 3

From the Temple to Homes

God's Dwelling Place in the Work of Luke

When Luke writes his two-volume work, his gospel and the book of Acts, the temple has already lain in ruins for several years. This alone would have been reason not to say much about the temple—that vestige of Judaism. Quite the opposite is true. With Luke the temple plays a role which is both entirely dominant and completely ambivalent. Luke places the city of Jerusalem and its temple at the center of his work but in two distinct phases: on the one hand he gives it prominent status, mainly at the beginning and end of the gospel; on the other hand, the role of the temple is supplanted, mainly in the book of Acts.

Everything Begins with the Temple

The stories of Jesus' childhood[1] begin and end in the temple. When the priest Zachariah takes up his duties in the temple in Jerusalem, the rota of tasks shared among the various priestly classes, he certainly does not suspect that he will receive a very unusual visit. Nevertheless it is right there in the temple that Gabriel, the angel

1. Luke 1–2.

of the Lord, appears to him to announce that he will soon become the father of John who will be charged with turning "the hearts of parents to their children, and the disobedient to the wisdom of the righteous, to make ready a people prepared for the Lord."[2] When it comes to the birth of a baby to a hitherto infertile couple, you would naturally imagine such long-hoped for news to be announced privately, not in the middle of a public ceremony, which was pretty impersonal when all is said and done. But Gabriel did not give his message to Elizabeth and Zachariah at home in the Judean mountains over a cup of tea or a cold drink. It is in the temple dwelling place of the divine presence, that the news is announced. And you could imagine that it took some time, in an age before mobile phones, for the news to reach Elizabeth, who after all was going to be the most directly affected.

Several months later, the temple again witnesses an important scene: the presentation of Jesus, firstborn son of Mary.[3] A quick reading might lead you to believe that this presentation is the natural and required thing to do. Luke, who seems to take great care to ensure that the gospel stories of the infancy of John and Jesus are strictly parallel, makes no mention of the presentation of John. This exception is significant. It underlines how important the temple is for Jesus. This is the place where Simeon and Anna's recognition of Jesus as messiah confirms the earlier witness of the shepherds in Bethlehem. Simeon is the first to affirm that his eyes have seen salvation, "a light for revelation to the Gentiles."[4] Then the prophetess Anna praises God and proclaims the child to all who are waiting for the liberation of Jerusalem.[5]

About twelve years later, Jesus is on a journey with his parents to celebrate the Passover.[6] You have no sense that the holy family makes the effort to travel because they think it important for the adolescent Jesus to participate in the festival. The fact that they

2. Luke 1:17.
3. Luke 2:21–24.
4. Luke 2:32.
5. Luke 2:38.
6. Luke 2:41–52.

do not make him the center of attention shows that his parents were not expecting anything special from this trip. But there is an undeniable tension between their attitude and that of Jesus. "Why were you searching for me? Did you not know that I must be in my Father's house? But they did not understand what he said to them."[7] The complete incomprehension recorded here is a sign of the impossibility for humans to grasp exactly who Jesus is and what his mission will be. True understanding of this comes only with the Holy Spirit. It is exactly because it surpasses our ability to understand that Luke takes so much trouble to convince his audience.

The Long Road to the Temple

Everything began in Jerusalem in the temple. Everything will end in the temple, for once Jesus has ascended to heaven, his disciples return to Jerusalem with great joy in their hearts: "they were continually in the temple blessing God."[8] Between the point of departure and this moment of arrival, between chapter 9 and the end of his gospel, Luke records no less than six times that Jesus is on the road to Jerusalem.[9] The last two references convey the idea of an ascent to the Holy City.[10] This is the hill-climb to salvation and the summit is in the temple. Hardly has Jesus arrived in triumph in the city than he installs himself every day in the building to teach. "All the people were spellbound by what they heard."[11] He will only leave this place at the time of his passion. "Every day he was teaching in the temple, and at night he would go out and spend the night on the Mount of Olives, as it was called. And all the people would get up early in the morning to listen to him in the temple."[12] The

---

7. Luke 2:49–50.
8. Luke 24:53.
9. Luke 9:51, 53; 13:22; 17:11.
10. Luke 18:31; 19:28.
11. Luke 19:48.
12. Luke 21:37–38.

temple becomes the messianic zone, the classroom where the great rabbi gives his teachings. The merchants have been chased away. Its status as a house of prayer has been restored.

Every Day in the Temple

There was no reason for the first Christians to shun the temple after the death and resurrection of Jesus. The place had been cleansed by the master. He had spent most of his last hours on earth there. You can imagine that out of pure nostalgia some of his disciples returned to the place where he uttered his last words of teaching. "Was it not under this very portico that Jesus taught us just a few days ago? Was it not here that he raised his voice against the scribes, Pharisees and Sadducees?" It's not surprise then that one reads these words from the pen of Luke: "Day by day, as they spent much time together in the temple . . ."[13] The first Christians had come up here just as Jesus had. But let us dwell for a moment on this practice for it would be interesting to know what exactly they were doing every day at the temple. The continuation of this text satisfies our curiosity.

The Temple as a Place of Prayer and Action

Nowhere in the book of Acts does reference to the temple indicate any sort of sacrificial practice. When Peter and John go up to the temple it is to pray. And this prayer is not mystical. It comes in response to human suffering. They have nothing to give the disabled man who is at the Beautiful Gate. But Peter has a hand to stretch out by which he enables him to get up.[14]

---

13. Acts 2:46.
14. Acts 3:1–10.

The Temple as a Place of Teaching

It is the imitation of their master which energizes the apostles. When everyone is eager for a miracle, Peter sets about preaching and teaching as Jesus had done in this same place not so very long ago. After all the stumbling and betrayals of the passion, the apostle and his colleagues have recovered. The coming of the Holy Spirit has lifted them. They no longer have bellies filled with fear. The efforts of the leaders, the elders, the scribes, and other senior priests to issue them a formal warning against speaking and teaching in the name of Jesus—all of this is entirely in vain.[15] They will not keep silent. And when they are thrown into the public prison they do not hesitate for a moment to obey the liberating angel who commands them to return to the temple to teach the people and tell them "the whole message about this life."[16] However after this episode Luke's account continues into another description which shows that the temple will never again play the same role: "As they left the council, they rejoiced that they were considered worthy to suffer dishonor for the sake of the name. And every day in the temple and at home they did not cease to teach and proclaim Jesus as the Messiah."[17] All it takes is a little word of three letters, a simple conjunction, for the hierarchy of places to tumble: in the temple *and* in the home. The temple classroom has become an impossible place thanks to the mean spiritedness of the religious authorities. But it matters little for God has never allowed himself to be contained by walls. God is going to turn over the page headed "Temple" to the one headed "Homes." But he does not do it without clearly saying why.

Stephen—The Temple Gravedigger

It is always the same story. When the Jewish authorities wish to condemn someone whose teaching upsets them, they are short

---
15. Acts 4:1–22.
16. Acts 5:20.
17. Acts 5:41–42.

on evidence and turn to false witnesses. The line of argument is always the same: Stephen has something against the temple. The case is very flimsy but we have already seen it used before against Jesus. So why not Stephen, too?

So Stephen is arrested and summoned to explain himself. The literary form of his speech adopted by Luke provides a great historical fresco, like some which we find elsewhere. One thinks of *the book of Jubilees*, or the *Liber antiquitatum biblicarum* (Pseudo-Philo), or the *Testaments of the Twelve Patriarchs,* or the *Jewish Antiquities* by Flavius Josephus. This literary genre is not new. In each one, an author retells and interprets the history of his people, using for the most part the leading personalities. Stephen recounts the history of Israel highlighting Abraham, Joseph, Moses, and finally Solomon.

Three themes run through the speech. First, that of displacement or movement. It is in Mesopotamia that this quite amazing God appears to Abraham. From there the patriarch leaves for Haran. Then after the death of his father, God leads him to "this land" but without giving him any inheritance, without giving him ownership of anything. Joseph, sold by the jealous patriarchs, is taken down into Egypt. His family, all seventy-five of them, join him there. But at the death of Jacob, they all move to Shechem to bury him in the tomb bought by Abraham. Moses in turn has to flee to the land of Midian after he has murdered an Egyptian. Having returned to Egypt, he leads his people out but they reject God and their hearts turn again to Egypt. It is only with David and then Solomon that this repeated migration comes to an end. Is this preoccupation with place the doing of God? I will revisit this later.

The second theme is that of exile. God speaks clearly to Abraham: his progeny will be exiled in a foreign land; they will be reduced to slavery and suffer ill treatment for four hundred years. Moses, too, as we have seen, will be exiled in Midian for forty years.

The third and last theme is that of idolatry. A short phrase appears twice to express this sinister deviation: the work of their own hands, or that which is the product of human hands.[18] The

18. Acts 7:41, 48.

first time it describes the manufacture of the golden calf, at the time when Moses seems to have disappeared for good on Mount Horeb. The second reference strangely enough is to the building of the temple by Solomon. In a way hitherto unheard of, Stephen likens the building of the holy structure on Mount Zion to an act of idolatry. The literal translation of verses 47 and 48 leaves no room for doubt: "But it was Solomon who built a house for him. Yet the Most High does not dwell in houses made with human hands. For this dwelling a divine hand is needed. 'Did not my hand make all these things?'"[19] The end of the speech drives home the point: "You stiff-necked people, uncircumcised in heart and ears, you are forever opposing the Holy Spirit, just as your ancestors used to do."[20] You're idolaters like your fathers were. Rebels like your fathers were. Murderers just like your fathers. Murderers indeed. The second murder now but for the same temple offence: first Jesus, then Stephen.

Cast your mind back to our comment on the building of the temple by Solomon. "For better or worse." Now we see it was definitely "for worse."[21] Over against this permanent temple which is certainly not the work of God, Stephen sets the tent of testimony. Marguerat puts it very well:

> The sort of dwelling most favored by God is a type of building which is on the move. So, the God of the forefathers is the God of the exodus, the God of the Way, one who cannot be pinned down, and this God is willing to go into exile.[22]

Once again God ups stakes and moves: he leaves the temple in Jerusalem. He is going to settle in a house or rather in any number of houses.

---

19. Acts 7:47–50.
20. Acts 7:51.
21. See above, the end of Itinerary 6, first part.
22. Marguerat, "Du temple à la maison," 306 (translation mine).

From the Temple into Homes

AFTER THE MURDER OF Stephen, the word "temple" disappears almost completely from the Gospel of Luke. He will use it again at the end of the book on the occasion of the conflict between Paul and certain Jews. It is the same old story of the Jewish opposition to Christians: "Fellow Israelites, help! This is the man who is teaching everyone everywhere against our people, our law, and this place."[23] This time however it is the Jews from Asia who create the conflict. They had certainly not been there in Jerusalem to hear Stephen's speech and they could not have learnt the argument against the temple from their brothers in Jerusalem. But they were simply proud like all ignorant men. Quite sure of their truth? Absolutely. In their stupidity and stubbornness, a decision was reached whose significance the decision-makers themselves have evidently not recognized. As Paul is arrested and dragged outside the temple, "immediately the doors were shut."[24] What a good decision they made to close the temple. For Luke the significance of their action is clear. The temple, whose role and importance he has been at pains to point out from the beginning of his work, has now become the place where the rejection of the Messiah and hostility to the good news gather force. So houses take the place of the temple. The word "house" now enters into Luke's lexicon to designate the substitute venue, the new center of the budding of Christianity. The use of the words "temple" and "house" in Acts is very revealing: "The vocabulary of the temple and the house unfolds in reverse symmetry."[25] Yesterday, it was the temple; today, it is houses.

When you look closely at how the book of Acts is constructed, you notice that it begins and ends in a house. Luke's gospel on the other hand, opens and closes in the temple.

The founding act of Christian mission takes place in a house; that is where the Spirit comes. It is true that the raining down of

---

23. Acts 21:28.
24. Acts 21:30.
25. Marguerat, "Du temple à la maison," 288.

From the Temple to Homes

tongues of fire, the loud noise like the blowing of a violent wind, all this taking place in the temple precincts, near to Solomon's portico, that would have been quite a show. Could there have been a better place to attest to the credentials, the seriousness, and the divine origin of this fledgling religious movement which witnessed to the fact that God had taken up residence on earth? The temple would have been the dream setting as far as marketing and communication are concerned. But it is not the place chosen by God! No. Right from the start it was in a house that the action took place. It was such an insignificant house that men passed it by, men who are normally so quick to build imposing religious shrines and preserve their traditions in marble. So where is this famous upper room in Jerusalem? Certainly not at the site usually shown to modern pilgrims! It has disappeared without trace, for at the time nobody thought anything of a tiny room occupied by a few cranks gathered to remember their departed hero.

It is in another house, in another town, that the book of Acts ends: Paul "lived there two whole years at his own expense and welcomed all who came to him, proclaiming the kingdom of God and teaching about the Lord Jesus Christ with all boldness and without hindrance."[26] Here Paul is in his own home in Rome. Paul is teaching here. It is a temple open to all. He is like his master, Jesus, who would teach in the temple and who, you will recall, made it into a "house of prayer."

In between this house at the beginning and the other at the end, other houses figure prominently in the book of Acts. Among them, the terrace on the house where Peter has the vision of the sheet suspended from heaven. Here is another turning point for Christianity which till then has been inclined to fall back into old habits of excluding people. And yet it is on this terrace, just like any other terrace of any other house of the period, that the barriers designed to protect the purity of the people of God are overturned.[27] Then another house, the one belonging to Lydia, the seller of purple from Thyatira. First of all, it is in the open air,

26. Acts 28:30–31.
27. Acts 10:9–43.

down by the river in Philippi, that she hears the preaching of Paul. But no sooner has she been baptized than she opens her home and asks Paul and his helpers to stay there.[28] "The divine presence in Acts does not manifest itself in a dwelling-place, a centralized venue, but in the impulse of the Spirit ... The house, trademark of fledgling Christianity, has made the Spirit accessible to everyone, everywhere."[29]

David, and Solomon even more, had hoped so much that their temple would become the center of the universe, the place on which all the pilgrims in the world would converge. With the passage of time, their dream turned into a nightmare. Could they in their wildest imagination have believed that in place of the magnificent building set on Mount Zion, the same God would have chosen to live in modest homes, invited by converted people, scattered here and there all over the world?

---

28. Acts 16:11–15.
29. Marguerat, "Du temple à la maison," 317 (translation mine).

ITINERARY 4

The "Epistle" to the Hebrews
or, Invitation to Enter the Sanctuary

OF ALL THE WRITINGS in the New Testament the "book" that is commonly referred to as the Epistle to the Hebrews is undoubtedly the one which refers most frequently to the sanctuary, to the temple, to the priesthood and all the sacrificial practices. At first sight, this document is not easy. Written in a refined form of Greek which is by far the best in the New Testament, it demands of the reader a good knowledge of the cultic practices of the Old Testament. Many venerable figures, most notably Martin Luther, have not really appreciated the subtleties of this text, which struggled to take its proper place among those books recognized as being inspired. Is it worthwhile today struggling with a document which is so far removed from our contemporary concerns? The great Charles Spurgeon in his early years did not have the best memories of Hebrews:

> I have a lively, or rather deadly, recollection of a certain series of discourses on the Hebrews, which made a deep impression on my mind of a most undesirable kind. I wished frequently that the Hebrews had kept the Epistle to themselves, for it sadly bored a poor Gentile lad.[1]

1. Spurgeon, *Early Years*, 48.

Hebrews is certainly a complex text, but it entirely deserves its place in the New Testament canon because what it says is quite extraordinary. But to hear it well, you must open your ears.

A Sermon Worth Listening To

When I say "open your ears," I mean it literally and figuratively. Let us be clear it is not a letter that we are dealing with here. It neither begins nor ends as a letter would have done.[2] Hebrews is a speech, or rather a homily or a sermon. Generally speaking, you do not read a sermon, you listen to it. Hebrews was constructed and composed as something to be heard. I can imagine the author himself, facing his audience, delivering his message like a great orator, according to the rules of rhetoric of his time. It would have lasted about fifty minutes.

In oral communication you have to seize the attention of the audience quickly, and make it quite clear what the subject is going to be. Then you have to keep underlining the heart of your message by means of repetition. Right from the beginning of the sermon, the preacher contrasts the word addressed in former times to their forefathers by the prophets with the word now spoken by Jesus, the Son:

> He is the reflection of God's glory and the exact imprint of God's very being, and he sustains all things by his powerful word. When he had made purification for sins, he sat down at the right hand of the Majesty on high, having become as much superior to angels as the name he has inherited is more excellent than theirs.[3]

The work of the Son is described in detail. He has made possible the purification of sins. He is seated in heaven. Further the purification of sins is a specific act, which is never in the hands of the ordinary believer. Only the priest, or rather the high priest, can

---

2. The last words (Heb 13:20–25) have been added to the sermon when it was sent in its written form.

3. Heb 1:3–4.

preside over the purification of sins. From the very beginning of his sermon, the author affirms three key ideas to his hearers:

- In these last days, there arises a priest, a high priest, who is the Son;
- He has truly washed away all sins;
- He is seated at the right hand of God.

This declaration will become the enduring refrain of the sermon, the pivotal point around which the sermon revolves. It is based mainly on two verses from Psalm 110:

> "Sit at my right hand
> until I make your enemies your footstool."[4]
> "You are a priest forever according to the order of Melchizedek."[5]

This two-verse refrain reappears in various shapes and forms right through to the end of the homily, as the following list clearly shows:

- "Sit at my right hand until I make your enemies a footstool for your feet?" (1:13)
- "You are a priest forever, according to the order of Melchizedek." (5:6)
- "having been designated by God a high priest according to the order of Melchizedek." (5:10)
- "where Jesus, a forerunner on our behalf, has entered, having become a high priest forever according to the order of Melchizedek." (6:20)
- "Now if perfection had been attainable through the Levitical priesthood—for the people received the law under this priesthood—what further need would there have been to speak of another priest arising according to the order of Melchizedek, rather than one according to the order of Aaron?" (7:11–12)

4. Ps 110:1.
5. Ps 110:4.

- "For it is attested of him, 'You are a priest forever, according to the order of Melchizedek.'" (7:15–17)
- "Now the main point in what we are saying is this: we have such a high priest, one who is seated at the right hand of the throne of the Majesty in the heavens." (8:1–1)
- "But when Christ had offered for all time a single sacrifice for sins, 'he sat down at the right hand of God,'" (10:12)
- "looking to Jesus the pioneer and perfecter of our faith, who for the sake of the joy that was set before him endured the cross, disregarding its shame, and has taken his seat at the right hand of the throne of God." (12:2)

There is no other book in the New Testament which refers more than once to the same text of the Old Testament. The first reference to Psalm 110 comes thirty seconds after the beginning of the homily, and then there are four others in the first twenty minutes.[6] Between 7:11 and 8:2, Psalm 110 is heard four times in less than five minutes. At most there are never more than eleven minutes between two references to it. It functions then very much as a refrain, a device highly favored in oral culture. This refrain captures the heart of the homily: Jesus is the priest / high priest who is seated at the right hand of God having completed the cleansing of sins. It is impossible to think of such work being done except in a sacred place, a temple or a sanctuary. We are then eager to discover the place of this ministry of purification led by this new priest/high priest. But before coming to that, it is worth just understanding why this sermon was delivered and what audience it was delivered to.

Masters of Decay

A refrain or repetition is important in all oral communication. But among other characteristics of orality[7] we must mention what is

---

6. Cf. Heb 1:13; 5:6, 10; 6:20.
7. Ong, *Orality*, 36–57, for the main characteristics of orality.

called the "agonist" aspect. "Agonistics" was for the ancients that part of gymnastics which had to do with combat between athletes. In oral performance, there is no fear of having a physical head-on confrontation with the audience. Rather it is a matter of the author challenging his audience. The incident in Antioch where Paul and Peter confront each other is a very good example of agonistics. Paul opposes his colleague quite openly,[8] using what is, at the very least, a muscular understanding of good fraternal Christian manners! The sermon to the Hebrews takes the same approach. The author lays into his audience, and does so directly and openly, and lands some fearful blows—for several reasons.

First of all it is clear that he thinks they should have been leaders, teachers. Instead, they are "bald on the inside of their heads" to use Jacques Prevert's witty phrase. "You have become dull in understanding," the audience is told. "For though by this time you ought to be teachers, you need someone to teach you again the basic elements of the oracles of God. You need milk, not solid food; for everyone who lives on milk, being still an infant, is unskilled in the word of righteousness."[9] It makes you think of certain regions in Europe which have very well-established reputations for slowness! But here this flaw has become much more serious: they have become casual, spiritually flabby, "they are crucifying again the Son of God and are holding him up to contempt."[10] They are complete wimps. This lack of rigor leads to heresy.

The reproach "they are crucifying again the Son of God and are holding him up to contempt"[11] is not easy to grasp. But at the very least we can understand that the house is in serious peril if it crucifies Jesus over again and dishonors him in the public square. A bit further on in the sermon, the author will speak about trampling on the Son of God.[12] So it is repeating the death of Jesus which creates the problem. To crucify again undoubtedly suggests that his

8. Gal 2:11–14.
9. Heb 5:11–13.
10. Heb 6:6.
11. Heb 6:6.
12. Heb 10:19.

first death did not seem to them to be sufficient as far as salvation was concerned, or to return to the beginning of the sermon, that for them the washing away of sins was not yet complete.

But who are the members of the audience? These flabby-minded types who ought to have been leaders but who have regressed to an infant state? Who are those who need to start all over from the beginning, taking into consideration those things difficult to explain? The book of Acts perhaps provides an answer to this question. "A great many of the priests became obedient to the faith."[13] What has become of these converts who hail from the priestly class? How can they be integrated into the early church? Strangely enough, neither the book of Acts—nor indeed any other book in the New Testament—gives them any place whatsoever in the Christian communities. It is the little people who sustain and guide but these former leaders do not appear to play any significant part at all. Are they considered as suspect? Maybe. Whatever the case, it is easy to imagine that after a time they began to miss the splendor of the temple, the grand ceremonies, and the festival celebrations, since the emerging Christian liturgy seemed much more simple. Prayer meetings, sessions for teaching in the sculleries of the houses were not in the same league as the routine in the temple on Mount Zion. Disappointment and disillusionment often make fertile soil for deviation and heresy.

You can understand why Hebrews places such emphasis on the priesthood, on the cleansing of sins, and on ancient cultic practices. The former priests are well placed to understand them. This sermon which is addressed to them is a translation of the gospel into their terms: Jesus is the priest / high priest. He has guaranteed the purification of sins. He is seated at the right hand of God in heaven. In heaven and not on earth. This sermon calls upon them to raise their heads and to cast off their this-worldly blinkers. This is not the time to listen to the siren voices of those Jews who wish to rebuild the temple or to kick-start the whole machine again. It is a whole different story—everything is possible through Jesus. "Hebrew priests, I have some really difficult things to say to you.

13. Acts 6:7.

Listen. This is a gymnastics lesson where I am going to stretch your slumbering muscles. It is going to hurt."

Warning: Demolition Site

Demolition sites where stretches of walls can collapse unexpectedly with unforeseen consequences are dangerous places. Wearing a hard hat is absolutely obligatory. Those listening to Hebrews had better wear a hard-hat, and the same applies to Christian readers too for the preacher is going to perform a demolition.

Suppression of the Levitical Priesthood

"Now if perfection had been attainable through the Levitical priesthood—for the people received the law under this priesthood—what further need would there have been to speak of another priest arising according to the order of Melchizedek, rather than one according to the order of Aaron?"[14] The first priestly order, the Levitical priesthood has not achieved what it was supposed to achieve. Its shortcomings are listed:

- Human priests are as feeble as any other human being;
- Their priesthood is weak and ineffectual;
- Sinful priests are subject to every weakness.

Shadows and Copies of Priesthood

The priests offer worship in a sanctuary that is a "sketch and shadow" of the heavenly one.[15] The word "copy" does not have a positive ring to it today. Possessing a copy of something, or copying it, is often seen as an act to be ashamed of. Customs officers stand watch at the last door of an airport just before the exit to arrivals. It can

14. Heb 7:11.
15. Heb 8:5.

be costly to parade past them with copies of designer goods. As for "shadow," it is the opposite of light. Shadow is the place where sin lurks while truth bursts out into clear daylight. Here the place of worship links two fatal flaws: "copy" and "shadow." It is not even a copy of an original but a second-rate imitation. On the mountain, the audience is told, Moses saw nothing more than a model.

An Outdated Covenant Which Will Soon Completely Disappear

The covenant, which in the sermon to the Hebrews is the document which governs all worship practices, does not itself escape criticism. It is certainly not beyond reproach. The very fact that God talks about a "new covenant" makes the old covenant even older, before our very eyes. Its end is nigh. Let me offer a contemporary example by way of explanation. It is 4th November 2008. Many American people are in front of their televisions, awaiting the outcome of the presidential election. In the middle of the night, the confirmation comes: Barak Obama is elected president of the United States of America. But at this very moment who is president? It is still George Bush, the present incumbent. The American people must wait until 20 January 2009 before Barak Obama officially assumes office. But at this precise moment—4th November—the incumbent president has sustained a fatal blow, just like the old covenant. The exit door beckons—oblivion is as close as it is inescapable.

Ineffectual Sacrifices

And so to the next attack! "Gifts and sacrifices are offered that cannot perfect the conscience of the worshiper, but deal only with food and drink and various baptisms, regulations for the body imposed until the time comes to set things right[16] . . . In these

---

16. Heb 9:9–10.

sacrifices there is a reminder of sin year after year. For it is impossible for the blood of bulls and goats to take away sins."[17]

So even on the Day of Atonement when you are supposed to be restored to your lost purity and innocence, the sacrifices can do nothing to effect the purification of the supplicant. Many Christians try hard to trace a clear continuity between the sacrificial system of the Old Testament and the sacrifice of Jesus on the cross. Yet the sermon to the Hebrews, which makes the sacrificial system into its focus, far from seeing continuity rather sees discontinuity between these different sacrifices.

It is hard to imagine the terrible blow inflicted by the preacher on his Jewish hearers, probably made up mostly of priests. Their acceptance of Jesus as the Messiah of God had certainly made them move on but now their whole world simply collapses. If the preacher goes that far, it is because there is urgency. They are quite clearly tempted, in one way or another, to go into reverse. They are undoubtedly thinking about ways to restore ancient practices, not to supplant their new belief but to complement it and in their own minds complete it. Now that he has razed everything to the ground it is time for the speaker to start building again.

Now We Can Rebuild Everything

Another Priesthood—A New High Priest

In the place of the first priesthood flawed by human weakness, the preacher to the Hebrews substitutes another priesthood. Its founder is Melchizedek—a historical character about whom we know very little. By New Testament times and even before, he had become a symbolic figure. The Essenes venerated him as a nearly divine.[18] Jesus does not qualify for the priesthood because he does not belong to the tribe of Aaron. But because of his attachment to the priestly order of Melchizedek, based on the reference to Psalm 110, the way is open to him to enter this ministry. Moreover, this

17. Heb 10:3–4.
18. See, e.g., 11QMelch, from the Qumran library.

other priestly order is vastly superior to the Levite version. Did Melchizedek not bless Abraham thus demonstrating his superiority over both their forefather and the Levites? Unlike the old order of priests, Jesus

> is able for all time to save those who approach God through him, since he always lives to make intercession for them . . . For it was fitting that we should have such a high priest, holy, blameless, undefiled, separated from sinners, and exalted above the heavens. Unlike the other high priests, he has no need to offer sacrifices day after day, first for his own sins, and then for those of the people; this he did once for all when he offered himself unlike the other high priests . . . has no need to offer sacrifices day after day, first for his own sins, and then for those of the people; this he did once for all when he offered himself.[19]

One Sacrifice in Place of Many

In the place of sacrifices which have to be offered repeatedly and unceasingly, and which can do nothing to cleanse the conscience, a single sacrifice is offered, that of the high priest himself. This sacrifice, and this alone, can purify the conscience. It opens the way into the sanctuary which had hitherto remained firmly shut. It provides a way for believers to offer to God their own living worship. Jesus abolishes sin.[20] Yes—you heard correctly —it is precisely the abolition of sin that the preacher is affirming here rather than simply the forgiveness of sins. The abolition of sin is just like the abolition of the death penalty: nobody can in the future be taken to the guillotine because of his misdeeds. Not another single person will die because of the blemishes on their soul. It by no means follows that there will never be any more guilty parties. Absolutely the opposite is true: it is vital to abolish the death penalty because there will always be offenders! An extraordinary idea. An idea as absolute as

19. Heb 7:25–27.
20. Heb 9: 8, 9, 14, 24, 26.

it is radical. An utterance, unutterably incomprehensible, of divine grace. The love of God is overwhelming. Woe to anyone who tries by devious human argumentation tries to add a single modification to this act of abolition. An act of abolition which carried a get-out clause? It's unheard of!

A Covenant Based on Amnesia

Under the old system, the Day of Atonement functioned, according to Hebrews, as a reminder of the sins of the past year. The new covenant offers instead a kind of amnesia: "This is the covenant that I will make with them after those days, says the Lord: I will put my laws in their hearts, and I will write them on their minds"; he also adds, "I will remember their sins and their lawless deeds no more."[21]

Whoever who asks God for a private session to talk about his sins will hear the response from God: "What are you talking about? I had totally forgotten. I cannot see . . ."

Finally an Entry Ticket to the Heavenly Sanctuary

The vocabulary of "entry" or "access" is common in the sermon to the Hebrews. There is the long introduction about entering into God's rest where the preacher invokes the experience of the people of Israel in the wilderness. The phrase "They shall not enter my rest,"[22] acts as another sort of refrain. Following their unfaithfulness, the Israelites who left Egypt did not enter into God's rest, that is to say that they did not cross into the land which had been promised to them. They all died in the desert. However the promise of entering lives on. It is worth noting that the themes of rest and the building of the temple are frequently found together in both biblical and noncanonical literature. Thus David cannot build the temple because of endless wars. So, because he could not

---

21. Heb 10:16–17.
22. Heb 3:11; 4:3.

enjoy peace and rest in his relations with neighboring peoples, it was impossible for him to build the very temple in which he would have been able to enjoy the rest which comes from entering into the presence of God.

By contrast Jesus is able to gain access to any and every space. Thus "we have a great high priest who has passed through the heavens, Jesus, the Son of God."[23] So he has moved beyond the veil on our behalf like a forerunner or go-between.[24] Most importantly "he entered once for all into the sanctuary, not with the blood of goats and calves, but with his own blood, thus obtaining eternal redemption"[25] having gone through the tent which till then remained a dead end. But what is this place into which he has entered once and for all?

Here is the text which, more than any other, allows us to answer this question: "For Christ did not enter a sanctuary made by human hands, a mere copy of the true one, but he entered into heaven itself, now to appear in the presence of God on our behalf."[26] It is clear that this does not take place on earth but elsewhere, in heaven. The sanctuary which is not built with human hands can only be the sanctuary in heaven. Here then is confirmation of the belief in the existence of a heavenly sanctuary. But the text tells us more about it. The preacher to the Hebrews completes his description as follows:

- This is not entry into a sanctuary on earth;
- But rather it is entry into heaven itself;
- To appear before God on our behalf.

Hebrews 9:24 is wonderfully shaped, which comes as no surprise in Hebrews. The thought develops and is completed in a three-part sequence. This sanctuary, the setting for the ministry of Christ the high priest, is certainly not on earth. It is in heaven.

23. Heb 4:14.
24. Heb 6:20.
25. Heb 9:12. *Sanctuary* is a better translation than *holy place*.
26. Heb 9:24.

But the preacher here makes a decisive movement away from traditional ideas of cosmology. The sanctuary is not the same thing as heaven. His reasoning goes on until it encompasses the very presence of God. This verse comes to us in Greek of course. It was spoken in Greek but the Hebrew is never far away. When a Jewish listener hears "before God" (*lipneh Adonai,* in Hebrew) he immediately understands the presence of God. In other words, the preacher to the Hebrews demolishes any material understanding of the geography of heaven. Yes there is a sanctuary in heaven. Jesus has entered it. But this sanctuary should not be conceived as a building, as a space located in any geography. It is into the very presence of God that Christ has entered on our behalf. Far from simply being in a place, he is in divine company. And Christ's presence there very quickly prompts an urgent invitation:

> Therefore, my friends, since we have confidence to enter the sanctuary by the blood of Jesus, by the new and living way that he opened for us through the curtain (that is, through his flesh), and since we have a great priest over the house of God, let us approach with a true heart in full assurance of faith, with our hearts sprinkled clean from an evil conscience and our bodies washed with pure water.[27]

Come, come in. The entrance is wide open. Don't stay outside. Outside there is only noise, commotion, worry. Inside there is rest.

All pagans believe in the existence of a heavenly sanctuary. But Christians believe that in Jesus Christ they have received an entry ticket to more than a building in the sky. God the Father is inviting them. "Come on, come in. My house is wide open to you. Here with me, it is your home now too."

---

27. Heb 10:19–22.

ITINERARY 5

At Home with John

The Lord Goes Camping

JOHN IS ONE OF the last authors of the New Testament chronologically speaking. Over half a century elapses between the events that he records and the appearance of final and definitive form of the texts which are attributed to him. Contrary to what many people think, this gap gives a particular weight to John's witness. For the passage of time allows for the development of new perspectives. What may have seemed insignificant or incomprehensible or untrue immediately after the ascension of Jesus gradually begins to make sense. A comparison taken from recent history can throw some light on this. After the 11 September 2001 attacks on the twin towers in New York, an increased fear of nonconventional weapons took hold of the United States. The main purpose of American foreign policy was to convince its allies that Iraqi's possession of weapons of mass destruction was a considerable threat for the world. Inspectors were sent. Reports were produced. Many heads of government were convinced and joined the United States in the Iraqi war. Some countries resisted, among them Russia, Germany and France. All the opponents were somehow considered as "bad boys," supporting Saddam Hussein. But nothing serious was actually discovered in Iraq. As time passed on, it became clear that this reading of the evidence was nothing else than a pretext to start the war. As time passed, a new interpretation of these events prevailed.

The Samaritan Woman: Jesus Moves On to Unfamiliar Territory

In the early chapters of the Gospel of John, the Samaritan woman poses the very question that has occupied us from the beginning of this book: "Where exactly is the house of God?" Or in other words: "Where exactly are we to offer our worship to God?" Astonished as she was at first that a Jewish man should enter into a conversation with the Samaritan woman that she was, the heroine of the story quickly seizes on to the fact that this is not just anybody. After all, this complete stranger has just put his finger on her painful problem: five husbands plus one lover. Rather than being offended and upset by Jesus' unexpected intrusion into her private life, she moves easily on to religious territory. Her response is remarkable, astonishing even. "Sir, I see that you are a prophet."[1] When a prophet puts himself at your personal disposal it is time to ask some important questions. Where is the place where God lives? Where should you go to meet him and offer him the worship due to him? This is not a new question. It had troubled the Samaritans since the destruction of the alternative temple they had built on Mount Gerizim,[2] which towers over Sychar where she lives. Should they build another temple on the ruins of the one which was destroyed? Can they do without a temple and worship God without dedicating a specific building for the purpose? Or should they settle for going back to the temple in Jerusalem? None of the solutions is really viable. The Jerusalem faithful would never tolerate the Samaritans rebuilding their temple ruins. But the Samaritans had a really hard time managing without a religious focal point. Remember that, in their minds, without a temple, you

---

1. John 4:19.
2. See the interlude, above.

are, to all intents and purposes, in the wilderness, a place where God does not live. Returning to Jerusalem is out of the question. Strict rules prohibited access to the temple to all Samaritans. It is a complete dead-end for them. And Jesus hates dead ends.

> Woman, believe me, the hour is coming when you will worship the Father neither on this mountain nor in Jerusalem. You worship what you do not know; we worship what we know, for salvation is from the Jews. But the hour is coming, and is now here, when the true worshipers will worship the Father in spirit and truth, for the Father seeks such as these to worship him.[3]

But this reply, containing as it does a neither-nor, is not a contemporary politically correct evasion, far from it. What is being stated here is a fundamental truth of Christianity. It is the foundation stone, it is the key to the treasury of all Christian liturgy: there is a sacred space no more, whether on Mount Gerizim or on Mount Zion in Jerusalem. What counts is not the place but the worshippers. This is completely foreign territory for the people of the first century. God no longer abides inside the walls which men have erected. It is not the splendor of the buildings, not the symbolism and richness of the decoration, not the height of the nave which makes a place habitable in God's eyes. With this declaration, worship, all worship, becomes centered on the worshippers and worshippers alone, and all the architects of sacred places are made redundant! Their buildings were only part of the way in which the faithful expressed their faith and no longer a condition of doing so.

Three Days to Rebuild the Temple

In John's account, the expulsion of the sellers and money changers from the temple happens at a different time. The event no longer forms an introduction to Passion Week as it does in the synoptic gospels. It comes right at the beginning of the ministry of Jesus as a first openly public demonstration of his authority—the wedding at

3. John 4:19–23.

Cana of Galilee in chapter two being an essentially private affair. The recollection of the disciples, to which John makes reference, is of a "jealous passion" which consumes Jesus. John is fond of ambiguities. It is not that he himself necessarily enjoys being equivocal. What he is often doing is showing just how skilled Jesus is at being equivocal, at playing with words so as to convey a meaning beyond the obvious. The Jews demand a sign by which Jesus can demonstrate his authority. Apparently offering them a response, he calls on them to destroy the temple themselves. If they do destroy it, this they will see the sign, a restoration of the temple in just three days. "But," they say, "forty-six years—that is what it took just for the last restoration of the temple and you are talking about three days for rebuilding it from top to bottom? Who is this man saying that the rebuilding will be better? Who is this man saying it will be quicker?" At the time nobody understood Jesus. Nobody pressed the point. It is only after the resurrection that the "sign" took on its full and profound meaning. And so, we get John's comment: "But he was speaking of the temple of his body."[4] Here is a teaching fundamental to the Christian faith: you can destroy every temple, every church, every chapel, every sanctuary, all the altars and all the holy places. After all the vandalism is complete there will remain one temple which is indestructible, which is impregnable, which no storm can ever touch, which has no need of being restored or enlarged or embellished: the body of Jesus. This is far more radical than the invitation to move on to new ground which Jesus offered and later explained to the Samaritan woman. All sacred space is consigned to oblivion.

God Under Canvas

Now let me make a confession: tents, camping—they are not my thing. Caravans, or better camper vans, are an improvement. But living under canvas is not for me. I can see that it *is* good, however for children. They like to play camping in the garden for a couple of hours. God, however, does not seem to agree with me. In John's first majestic chapter where he lays the foundation of Christianity

---

4. John 2:21.

and tells us that the Word became flesh—right there nestles this magnificent verse, which for our purposes, must be written in gold: "And the Word became flesh and lived among us."[5] Theologians like this kind of phrase because, as it stands, it is really beyond our grasp. That leaves us with the feeling that we have the task of discovering and conveying the hidden meaning. Actually a more literal translation is sufficient: "The Word became flesh; the Word pitched his tent among us." God had said as much to David. He had repeated it to the prophets. He had never requested anyone to build a temple for him. The forty years in the desert where he had camped with his own people, in the midst of his people—none of that distressed him. No, he liked it. He liked being in among the crowd. He had no anxiety about his own fragility. There is suppleness, flexibility, and adaptability in this God. The hardness of the stone and marble, the opaqueness of heavy cloth—these do not appeal to him. On the other hand, the canvas of tents does not filter out the light. It lets it through. In Jesus of Nazareth, the Word in the form of a simple human being, in him God decided to come and live among his own. Amazing risk, indeed! How could it be that he, the God whom even the heavens cannot encompass, how could this God choose to be the camper among us? How could he do this just to ensure that he could be close, so very close, close enough for a rapid response to our every movement unhindered by the need rebuild every time? Modern tents can be erected in a couple of seconds, or so the advertising claims. A couple of seconds over against forty six years? No contest. Think about Zeus and all his fellow gods, those champions of thunder, strength, grandeur, they must laugh so much at this camper-God. He who laughs best laughs last. All their temples are in ruins, and where they are still standing, it is usually only because archaeologists have come upon them, rebuilt them, and restored them often at enormous cost. The fragile tent of this other God has braved the centuries, it is still there. And he is still there and still waiting, waiting for something more. The grand finale of the dwelling of God among human beings is still to come. For grand finale read divine finale.

5. John 1:14.

ITINERARY 6

The Temple of God in the Book of Revelation

THE BOOK OF REVELATION uses the word "temple" thirteen times—more than any other book in the New Testament. The author not only mentions the temple but also certain pieces of its furniture. The One who looks like a Son of Man, and who is clearly the main character in the book, appears in the midst of the seven lampstands.[1] Further on, the altar of incense and the censer are mentioned.[2] Later, the ark of the covenant makes an appearance.[3]

The temple is designated twice in Revelation as "the temple of God,"[4] the only times it gets that title in the New Testament. This sacred place is unquestionably the nerve center of the action in the book. It is from here that another angel leaves to proclaim that the time has come to reap a harvest on earth, that is, to gather in the elect. It is from here that another angel leaves to proclaim that it is time to pick the clusters of grapes, that is, to unfurl the wrath of God against the lost.[5] When the temple opens there emerge seven

---

1. Rev 1:12–13. See also Rev 2:1 and 11:4.
2. Rev 8:3–5 and 11:1.
3. Rev 11:19.
4. Rev 11:1, 19.
5. Rev 14:15–20.

angels who carry the plagues. It is from here that they receive the order to pour out on the earth the seven bowls of the wrath of God.[6]

This temple is like no other, for beside the usual furniture which reminds you of the temple in Jerusalem, you also find a throne,[7] which suggests to you that this place is a royal palace. On a first reading it would not be surprising to think of the temple in the Apocalypse as the place where God lives, a sort of divine headquarters. Then, when it opens up it unleashes a supernatural spectacular: "there were flashes of lightning, rumblings, peals of thunder, an earthquake, and heavy hail."[8] These are precisely the same signs which accompany the presence of God on Mount Sinai when he speaks to Moses to give him the law.[9] We find them once more when the seventh bowl is poured out over the earth.[10]

It would be easy to assume from these verses that there is a temple in heaven and that God lives in it. The place is not described, but the details emerging here and there in the text are sufficient to convince us that this "building" is very similar to the temple in Jerusalem. It is the same thing but of course bigger and better. A number of commentators have fallen into this interpretative trap, for trap is certainly what it is. How do we avoid being trapped? Only by remembering what the purpose of the book of Revelation is and looking at the means that the writer uses to achieve that purpose.

Revelation: A Literature of Crisis

The exile of the Israelites in Babylon in the sixth century BCE and their return to their country seventy years later brought with it nothing but disillusionment. The independence and power of

6. Rev 16:1.
7. Rev 16:17.
8. Rev 11:19. See also Rev 15:8.
9. Exod 20:18.
10. Rev 16:17.

the preexilic years had definitely disappeared. There was nothing much more to expect from the future. Only a great upheaval direct from the hand of God and the emergence of a totally different world, only this would reinstate the birthright to the people. It is in this dark context that the literature known as apocalyptic first emerges and develops, a genre of which the last book in the Bible is the crowning glory. It is a literature of crisis, where powers hostile to the people of God persecute and oppress them. They are all described as forms of the supreme enemy—the devil—who will be for all: the establishment of the reign of God, symbolized by the descent of the new Jerusalem.

The Revelation of Jesus Christ . . .[11]

In spite of the grim context out of which it grows, the book of Revelation is not entirely a list or calendar of events which must take place between now and the end of the world. Rather, it is the revelation of the person of Jesus, the Messiah, the one sent from God, very God made flesh. In itself, this revelation is an unveiling. What was hidden now appears in broad daylight. As readers, we take off the veil just as one unveils a work of art which an artist has just finished. What we unveil is God's final act in the cosmic drama.

. . . In a Most Unusual Language . . .

The revelation of Jesus Christ is nothing less than the revelation of God himself. But there is no grammar, no human vocabulary which can measure up to the challenge of expressing it. Words fail the author as he is called up into heaven itself.[12] He passes from this earth to a heavenly place. He is going to have to coin a new language to try and put within human grasp that which surpasses human understanding. Just like a poet, the author of the

11. Rev 1:1.
12. Rev 4:1.

Apocalypse piles symbol upon symbol to describe the person of Jesus and his actions as well as those of the forces ranged against him. And so there appears the lamb which is like no other lamb: upright, with seven horns and seven eyes, receiving the book out of the hand of God himself.[13] The depiction and juxtaposition of pictures make the language used extraordinary. The numbers have little to do with arithmetic: they express a universality on earth (four), fullness (seven), the people of God (twelve), and combine in multiples to reveal rich meanings; for example, the square of twelve multiplied by a thousand denotes what is quite clearly not an exact number—144,000 persons—but a gathering of all the elect (7:4–8; 14:4). The colors bear a message: white evokes purity and victory, red for murder and violence, black for impiety and death. All enemies are described in a terrifying manner: a dragon breathing red fire, with seven heads and ten horns.[14]

A Language Which Must Be Deciphered

In the Apocalypse it is vital not to take the words in their literal sense but to decode them. Otherwise the text becomes completely absurd. Do we imagine that that there literally is in heaven a lamb like the one described in the book?[15] Do we imagine that there is in heaven a woman, robed in the sun, who brings a child into the world?[16] Do we imagine that there is a prostitute in heaven?[17] And what shall we say of the four horses[18] or the two terrifying beasts?[19] Heaven cannot be this great phantasmagorical bazaar, which would make any Arab souk look pale by comparison. In the same way, in order to maintain an interpretation which is at all coherent, we must not think that when the Apocalypse speaks of a heavenly

13. Rev 5:6–7.
14. Rev 12:3.
15. Rev 5:6–7.
16. Rev 12.
17. Rev 17.
18. Rev 6.
19. Rev 13.

temple of God that it indicates an actual building which serves as both sacred space and royal palace. A last text confirms this in a most striking way.

God Is the Temple

At the time of the last judgment, which marks the end of all those who have opposed God, there in the text of the Apocalypse is the temple. But no sooner does John see a new heaven and a new earth[20] than the temple disappears for good from the text. When the angel shows him the heavenly Jerusalem adorned as a bride, John is astonished to find no temple in the city. He clearly states, "I saw no temple in the city, for its temple is the Lord God the Almighty and the Lamb."[21] This temple is not a place, or a building, but a person, or rather two persons: the Lord God, the Almighty, *and* the Jesus Christ, the lamb—the subject of the book. Should we be surprised? Not at all. For God has never asked anyone to build a temple for him. How could it make sense to build a temple in heaven when he had not wanted one on earth? How could he who has always preferred the vulnerability of a tent in the wilderness possibly be confined to a life lived between walls? He certainly has no need of a big office as his headquarters, with telephone, fax, computer, scanner, printer, and for good measure a white board for business meetings with his angels.

The time has surely come to put an end to all our fantasies about the heavenly universe. Our tentative constructions are all-too-human, and they naively confuse what is said with what is meant.

Between God and ourselves there are not and never will be any more windows, any more doors or walls, or thresholds to cross. There are no more steps to climb to the presence of God. God is there, in the midst of the city, just he was originally in the midst of the garden.

20. Rev 21:1.
21. Rev 21:22.

The book of Revelation, and with it the whole Bible closes with a promise which rings with certainty: "Surely I am coming soon."[22] It is the Son of Man, the Messiah, Jesus who is coming. You only have to go back a few lines in the text to find the same verb "come" used as an invitation. "The Spirit and the bride say, 'Come.'"[23]

If one does respond to the invitation, he/she will enter the temple of God. Do not expect to enter a building which is sumptuous and sublime. No. You will come into the presence of the God of the universe. The divine SatNav will have brought you home. You will at last have an answer to the original question: Where does God live? You will be a distinguished guest—at home with him, forever.

---

22. Rev 22:20.
23. Rev 22:17.

Journey's End

THERE IS A STORY of a customs and excise officer who, though corrupt, is called Mr. Clean. Yes, the name Zacchaeus means "one who is pure or purified." Maybe the Romans chose him because of his name, hoping that he would be a good civil servant, reliable and honest. For his job as a tax collector for the Roman Empire was not easy. Zacchaeus and his staff ruled the town of Jericho—an important oasis which was the communications hub between the East and the Mediterranean, and between Egypt and the North. The system they operated was a sort of franchise: they had the right to collect taxes on all goods entering and leaving the town. They funneled back the lion's share to Rome but extracted their own profit margin. A letter found in the imperial archives in Rome throws light on the practices of tax collectors. A senior Roman official is worried about their excessive profits. The traders who must pay these taxes are up in arms. Rome fears the worst and asks the customs and excise officers to be more moderate and reasonable in the tariffs which they impose. So Zacchaeus is no philanthropist. His goal is to make a profit, a healthy profit like every other tax collector.

Luke is not unaware of the way these Roman stooges abuse the system. Indeed every time he uses the word "customs and excise officer" he adds the word "sinner" as if there was no better way of defining a sinner than to point to these tax collectors.[1] And he

1. See, e.g., Luke 5:30; 7:34; 15:1, 2.

describes John the Baptizer, preaching just three or four kilometers from Jericho, and telling those who wish to be baptized very clearly to demand no more than is reasonable.[2]

Mr. Clean—Zacchaeus—hears one day that Jesus is coming to the town. So now, it is probably his staff of tax collectors who have given him the information. This man Jesus who everyone is talking about, is coming to town—it is a moment not to be missed. Just to put a face to the name Messiah.

But at less than one meter sixty, he is going to have difficulty seeing Jesus. So we find the "big" boss of customs and excise, Zacchaeus, perched in his sycamore tree. He was not beyond the range of Jesus's gaze but he was too high up to be able to actually meet him. So Jesus told him, "Zacchaeus, come down quickly."[3] The attempt by Zacchaeus to remain *incognito* has failed. He does not understand yet that there is nowhere where you can hide from God's searching eyes. "Come down quickly." It is the sort of thing that you would say to a child up in a tree who you thought was in some danger. But "come down quickly, I want to come to your house today" sounds like a different proposition altogether.

What must he have thought? Jesus is actually inviting himself to his house, to the house of Mr. Clean-and-Dirty. I can imagine the fear that must have filled Zacchaeus for a moment. For tax collectors are trained to be suspicious and intrusive. Could this visit be a search of his premises? Given his ways of working, Zacchaeus had every reason to fear a one-to-one encounter.

Anyway Zacchaeus comes down quickly—everything moves fast in this story. Here he is, at home playing host to Jesus, the Messiah of God. It is what follows in this story which provides the best possible conclusion to this book:

> So he hurried down and was happy to welcome him. All who saw it began to grumble and said, "He has gone to be the guest of one who is a sinner." Zacchaeus stood there and said to the Lord, "Look, half of my possessions, Lord,

---

2. Luke 3:12, 13.
3. Luke 19:5.

Journey's End

I will give to the poor; and if I have defrauded anyone of anything, I will pay back four times as much."[4]

When Jesus is with Zacchaeus his whole life is turned completely upside down. Then and only then, Zacchaeus, Mr. Filthy-Dirty, becomes Mr. Squeaky-Clean. Everything changes radically. Zacchaeus, the shady customs officer, the corrupt civil servant, who through other people's labor fills his own pockets, he with the terrible reputation, he of all people decides to give half of all he owns to the poor and to restore fourfold the amounts that he has extracted unlawfully. All because Jesus came to see him! Can you imagine a conversation around the fireplace in the evening between Zacchaeus and Jesus:

> Well, Zacchaeus have you had a good day?
> Oh yes Lord, I conned a caravan of Bedouins who wanted to pass through Jericho. I tell you, I really cleaned them out.
> Well done, Zacchaeus. Let's raise a glass to your success.

Can you imagine that? I certainly cannot. For if Jesus lives in this house—or any house for that matter—he changes its values, its practices, its lifestyle, its habits. It is the radical change announced by John the Baptizer. It is the sole condition for salvation in Christianity, the divine living together with the human.

So when all is said and done, where does God live? There is no single answer to this question. For, as we have seen, throughout history, God has never stopped moving on, obsessed as he is with following his children, being close to them, as close as possible: first in the garden, then by altars, in sanctuary and temple, in the human body, in the community of believers, in their houses. Above all, God has chosen in the person of Jesus to set up camp among human beings. The story of Zacchaeus shows this final stage, which is without doubt the most important. Rather than ask believers to go and meet him in a temple, whatever that might be, wherever that might be, God comes to us in Jesus Christ. He

---

4. Luke 19:6–8.

wishes to come and live with each of us, individually, just as he did with Zacchaeus. His presence with us transforms us, it gives health, it gives life.

To all of today's Mr. and Mrs. Uncleans, Jesus says: "I must come to live with you today. If you want your life to change, if you really want to empty your pockets of every sort of ill-gotten gain, if you want to do away with your shady tax collectors' tricks, whatever they might be, then let me come in."

Obviously it is a lot less risky to build temples, cathedrals, breathtaking holy places where you can park God in solemn and majestic style. You can build places where you pay a visit more or less regularly. It is easier to have a "rent-a-God." You can rent him in the same way that you rent a holiday apartment. Just for the weekend. Afterwards you can go home, duty done, just as you might visit your elderly parents in an old-peoples' home.

If we treat God like this, our lives continue. Just as they were before, and, we think, just as they always will be. And our pockets fill up, and empty just as fast. And we ask God to help us to change . . . but we keep him still shut away in our temples and sanctuaries. But God never gives up. Still he knocks at the door seeking to come in.

"Come down quickly, he continues to say and says again today, you, you are my temple."

And the voice on the GPS says: "You have reached your destination."

Bibliography

Boda, Mark J., and Jarnie Novotny, eds. *From the Foundations to the Crenellations: Essays on Temple Building in the Ancient Near East and Hebrew Bible*. Alter Orient und Altes Testament 366. Münster: Ugarit-Verlag, 2010.

Bogaert, Pierre-Maurice. "La demeure de Dieu selon Jérémie et Ezékiel: La Maison, l'Exil ou la Ville." In *Quelle maison pour Dieu?*, edited by Camille Focant, 209–28. Lectio Divina. Paris: Cerf, 2003.

Bruce, Preston P. "Inscription of Nabopolassar No III, col. Ii, 5–20." *American Journal of Semitic Languages and Literatures* 16 (1900) 186.

Charlesworth, James H., ed. *The Old Testament Pseudepigrapha*. 2 vols. New York: Doubleday, 1983.

Collectanea Papyrologica: Texts Published in Honor of H.C. Youtie. Bonn: Habelt, 1976.

Clark, Kenneth. "Worship in the Jerusalem Temple after A.D. 70." *NTS* 6 (1959/60) 269–80.

Diodorus Siculus. *Library of History*. Vol. 10. Translated by Russel M. Geer. Loeb Classical Library. Cambridge: Harvard University Press, 1989.

Eliade, Mircea. *Cosmos and History: The Myth of the Eternal Return*. New York: Harper & Row, 1959.

Focant, Camille. *The Gospel according to Mark*. Eugene, OR: Pickwick, 2012.

Garcia Martinez, Florentino, and Eibert J. C. Tigchelaar, eds. *The Dead Sea Scrolls*. Study ed. 2 vols. Leiden: Brill, 1997–98.

Genesis Rabbah. In *The Midrash Rabbah*, vol. 1. London: Soncino, 1977.

Grappe, Christian, and Alfred Marx. *Le sacrifice: Vocation et subversion du sacrifice dans les deux testaments*. Geneva: Labor et Fides, 1998.

Hallo, William H. *The Context of Scripture: Monumental Inscriptions from the Biblical World*. Vol. 2. Leiden: Brill, 2000.

Hundley, Michael B. *Gods in Dwellings: Temple and Divine Presence in the Ancient Near East*. Atlanta: SBL, 2013.

Isaacs, Marie E. *Sacred Space: An Approach to the Theology of the Epistle to the Hebrews*. JSNTS 73. Sheffield: Sheffield Academic, 1992.

Bibliography

Koester, Craig R. *The Dwelling of God: The Tabernacle in the Old Testament, Intertestamental Jewish Literature and the New Testament*. Catholic Biblical Quarterly Monograph Series 22. Washington: Catholic Biblical Association of America, 1989.

Louw, Johannes Peter, and Eugene A. Nida, eds. *The Greek English Lexicon of the New Testament: Based on Semantics Domains*. New York: United Bible Societies, 1988.

Marguerat, Daniel, and Yvan Bourquin. *How to Read Bible Stories: An Introduction to Narrative Criticism*. London: SCM, 1999.

Marguerat, Daniel. "Du Temple à la maison suivant Luc-Actes." In *Quelle maison pour Dieu?*, edited by Camille Focant, 285–317. Lectio Divina. Paris: Cerf, 2003.

Marx, Alfred. *Les systèmes sacrificiels de l'Ancien Testament*. Vetus Testamentum 105. Leiden: Brill, 2005.

Ong, Walter. *Orality and Literacy*. London: Routledge, 1982.

Porten, Bezalel, J. Joel Farben, Cary J. Marin, Günter Vittmann, eds. *The Passover Letter: The Elephantine Papyri in English*. Leiden: Brill, 2011.

Porten, Bezalel, and Ada Yardeni, eds. *Textbook of Aramaic Documents from Ancient Egypt*. Vol. 1. Jerusalem: Hebrew University, 1986–99.

Rück, Jan. "Une dynastie en crise: la promesse dynastique en 2 Samuel 7 comme reaction à l'exil." *Transeuphratène* 42 (2012) 81–97.

Spurgeon, Charles H. *The Early Years, 1834–1859*. Edinburgh: Banner of Truth, 1962.

Stroumsa, Guy. *The End of Sacrifice: Religious Transformations in Late Antiquity*. Chicago: University of Chicago Press, 2009.

www.ingramcontent.com/pod-product-compliance
Lightning Source LLC
Chambersburg PA
CBHW071505150426
43191CB00009B/1427